New Fiction

ECHOES ON THE WIND

Edited by

Kelly Oliver

First published in Great Britain in 2005 by
NEW FICTION
Remus House,
Coltsfoot Drive,
Peterborough, PE2 9JX
Telephone (01733) 898101
Fax (01733) 313524

SB ISBN 1 85929 121 X

FOREWORD

When 'New Fiction' ceased publishing there was much wailing and gnashing of teeth, the showcase for the short story had offered an opportunity for practitioners of the craft to demonstrate their talent.

Phoenix-like from the ashes, 'New Fiction' has risen with the sole purpose of bringing forth new and exciting short stories from new and exciting writers.

The art of the short story writer has been practised from ancient days, with many gifted writers producing small, but hauntingly memorable stories that linger in the imagination.

I believe this selection of stories will leave echoes in your mind for many days. Read on and enjoy the pleasure of that most perfect form of literature, the short story.

Parvus Est Bellus.

Contents

JPEG AND GIF

Ron Whatley

Ex rock musicians, Pete Durrant and Roy Daner, whose turbulent careers began in the 60's before finishing somewhat ignominiously in 2000, following a Seaford pub gig that turned violent, are rumoured to be meeting up again after four years. But don't hold your breath, folks. The rock Methuselahs have no plans to make any more music since their last album, 'Higher Than Sky', released in 1998. Pete Durrant has said that he would like to try to build bridges with his ex partner. Over troubled waters, Pete? ... Rolling Stone.

When Durrant entered the busy lounge of the Imperial Hotel in Tenby, Pembrokeshire, he could see that Roy Daner had arrived. He'd managed to secure a window table and was busy scouring the sea visage outside. An empty cup was before him.

'Well, at least you actually turned up, mate,' Pete growled from the bar, where he had stopped to order coffee.

Daner, recognising the familiar South London accent, turned his head. 'Bora da - look what the cat's just dragged in,' he drawled. His weathered face was creased in a grin of welcome.

'What's all this 'bora da' business, then?' Pete growled. 'Have you gone native or something?'

'It's Welsh - I think it means good day - something like that. Anyway, where are you staying, old buddy?'

'Right here! You know damn well - you booked the room for me,' Pete snapped. Already his old music partner was beginning to bug him - just like in the old days of gigging.

Daner pursed his lips. 'Yeah, so I did,' he said with a smirk. 'And you look like someone with plenty of dosh to flash about so how about making that another coffee for me, and see if that tart behind the counter can rustle up a doughnut as well ...'

Pete grimaced, but relayed the order to the counter assistant - a hard-eyed blonde. She shook her head. Pete paid for the coffees. He was a stocky man of medium height. He had a craggy face, dark smouldering eyes and his grey hair was close cropped. Overall, he looked as though he could handle himself in a roughhouse, old as he was: no flab bulging from the smart grey suit he wore. He carried the coffees across to where

Daner was sitting. 'Fresh out of doughnuts,' he grumped as he set the cups down onto the table.

Daner pulled a face and shrugged. 'So, why are you dressed up like a ponce, old buddy?' he questioned.

'It's about looking respectable - unlike you.'

'Whatdya mean?' Roy Daner seemed affronted. He brushed back untidy grey locks of hair from his forehead.

'Well, just look at you - mutton dressed as lamb: distressed leather bomber; dirty, mauve 'Grateful Dead' T-shirt. And those disgusting jeans you're wearing - rips all over the legs.' Pete flicked some imaginary fluff from the lapels of his suit jacket. His one concession - this morning - to any show of informality, was a pristine white shirt open at the neck. Actually he felt prissy and uncomfortable in the outfit, preferring jeans and T-shirts himself, but his thinking had been to try to get one over on his old Nemesis, Roy Daner.

'Cut the crap, Pete. You're just showing off. Anyhow, I'll dress how I please - it shows how broke I am. All I'm interested in is revenue from our Greatest Hits Compilation. The moula will come in very handy to augment my state pension.'

Pete sipped coffee, his face a mask. 'You know it didn't happen,' he said at length. 'There's nobody interested in showcasing our retro stuff.'

'Wha…?' Roy Daner contorted his leathery features into a look resembling surprise. His blue eyes were open wide, staring. With his untidy hair standing out at crazy angles from his head, he could have been a contender for a Nutty Professor.

'I e-mailed you all the details: you should try reading them instead of messing about with those flight simulation programmes. There's no more mileage in a couple of old, has-been rock musicians - even if we did make the charts a few times.'

'Sixties to late nineties - we were superstars - at least for some of the time,' Daner declared aggressively.

'Not anymore. We're dead and buried according to the media. Count your blessings. At least we still have a dribble of royalties being paid to us …'

'Some consolation.' Roy's eyes were narrowed under beetling eyebrows. His mind was working harder than a Fender Telecaster.

Pete sat back and drank coffee. He said nothing; knew the way his old music partner's mind operated. Eventually, Daner would evolve some cockeyed plan, comprised of illogic and lunacy and that could mean bad news for both of them. At best they might just escape with their lives. That pub gig in 2000 was a case in point.

'I've got it,' Roy said excitedly, clicking the fingers of both hands, almost knocking over his full cup of coffee. Then he relapsed into pregnant silence again.

Pete shook his head from side to side, wondering if it had been such a good idea to respond to Roy's request for this meeting. The distance alone had been off-putting enough. Pete resided in Brighton, running a second-hand book business in Seaford, while Roy now lived in Pembrokeshire, Wales. Certainly Pete's wife, Suzie, hadn't been too keen on him making the trip. She had too many bad memories of Roy's irreverent behaviour in the past to contend with.

'Yeah, that's it.' Roy surfaced from the depths of thought again. 'We'll go on the road again. It'll be like the good old days - when Dee and Dee were touring.'

'No. No.' Pete protested so loudly that several other patrons nearby turned to look at him. Bad memories were flooding back: smelly transit vans loaded with musical instruments; empty vindaloo cartons; long hours spent travelling from gig to gig along dark roads; no sleep; roadies; groupies; sweating buckets on stage before a screaming audience. Now, he could see it all for what it had been - a nightmare. 'Not on your life,' he said forcibly. He was shaking his head.

Roy Daner was grinning like an idiot. 'What's up, Pete? Your face has definitely got a green tinge to it,' he said gently, although there was little concern in his tone.

'Never again. I've told you enough times that I'm finished with rock 'n' roll, specially after that last concert of ours.' Pete spat out the words.

'But that was four years ago.'

'Whatever. The answer is still *no*,' Pete growled, adding, 'besides, we're far too old for that game; we're forgotten history.'

Roy Daner leaned back in his chair. He pursed his lips. 'I'm really disappointed in you,' he declared sadly. 'My old buddy, one of the finest rhythm guitarists in the country, who, like me, read Kerouac's, 'On The Road' - and answered the call - backing down from the adventure of a lifetime.'

'Jeez Roy, don't you ever give up? I'm sixty-eight years old ...'

'Ditto.'

‘I’ve got a wife and …’

‘So have I. What’s the problem?’

‘You still don’t get it, Roy. We’re over the hill …’

‘Hey, hold your horses. I’m not that far gone that I can’t still appreciate a nice bit of skirt,’ Roy proclaimed loudly, causing a tweedy brunette at an adjacent table to glare at him. Roy didn’t care. He continued to bang on relentlessly. ‘And, if memory serves me correctly, old buddy, you weren’t averse to female company yourself - especially when Suzie wasn’t in the frame to rein you in …’

‘Out of order. That was below the belt, Roy.’

Roy grinned. ‘Yeah, that was usually the place,’ he drawled.

‘The answer is still an emphatic *no.*’ Pete’s mind was made up. Nothing could influence him to change direction.

‘I respect only those who resist me; but I cannot tolerate them,’ said Roy gravely.

‘Who said that?’ questioned Pete.

‘Me. And before that, Charles De Gaule. Rather apt at this time, what?’ Daner had a look of pure delight on his worn features. He was thoroughly enjoying winding up his old music partner. Eventually, when he had savoured the moment, he chose to drop a verbal bombshell. ‘Of course, I didn’t really mean all that stuff about us actually going on the road again,’ he said. ‘Well, not in the physical sense …’

Pete sagged in his chair, nonplussed. ‘Run that by me again,’ he requested.

But, Roy, in his cups, could only plough onwards. ‘No, I was thinking about us travelling a ‘virtual’ road.’

‘Uh?’ said Pete, adding, ‘The greater our knowledge increases the more our ignorance unfolds.’

‘And who uttered those choice words?’ Daner liked playing word games.

‘John F Kennedy.’

‘And look what happened to him,’ said Roy dismissively. ‘Now listen up - we’re both into 21st century technology - why can’t we reinvent ourselves as a couple of cartoon characters? We could let them perform our retro rock ’n’ roll on the web. And we wouldn’t have to do much except market our well-aired musical goodies for anyone to download - for a fee, of course. That way we might still get to sell our Greatest Hits collection …'

Pete Durrant was taken aback by Roy's enthusiastic outpourings. Intuitively though, he was suspicious, even if the plan seemed outlandish enough to work - possibly. He felt duty bound to inject a note of pessimism. 'It won't get off the ground,' he declared grimly.

'Nonsense, of course it will,' Roy came back. 'I've already been researching the idea. A computer boffin-friend of mine is putting in time to design a possible website for us. All we need is a couple of eye-catching pseudonyms for our virtual doubles. You could be Bugs Bunny and I'll be the Road Runner …'

'I would certainly veto any suggestion about using the names Dee and Dee ever again,' said Pete, adopting a more conciliatory tone. He was thinking that Daner had always been a madman, but occasionally he had managed to pull off a good scam in the past.

Roy was excited and gushing with enthusiasm. 'I agree. Anyway, that part of our lives is over and done with. No, I reckon we ought to choose two 'names' that most computer-oriented, music down-loaders will recognise immediately …'

JPEG: Acronym for Joint Photographic Experts Group
GIF: Acronym for Graphics Interchange Format

No Wild Animals In The Cave

Joyce Walker

'But there were no wild animals in the cave,' the five-year-old boy said as I stopped the winch bringing him and his father to freedom in the west.

He sounded disappointed but I was pleased, as were the others who stood at the mouth of the tunnel on that night of October 3rd 1964. Wild animals in the form of the 'vapos', the East German border guards, were creatures we could do without.

Twenty-eight people came through the tunnel that night, blue-lipped and fighting for breath, who had to be rushed away instantly for medical attention.

I had good reason to be there, but even if I had not, their gratitude would have made all those weekends without sleep worthwhile and despite the exhaustion, if I was asked, I would do it all again.

While I waited I reflected on how it all began.

I had regarded it as something of a joke when my friend said he had been in contact with his family on the other side of the wall and that he believed the construction of a tunnel between East and West was possible. When, however, he managed to rent a disused bakery in Bernauer Strasse at a cost of DM100 per week and drew up the plans, I willingly agreed to help.

Others did too, thirty-six of us in all, some like me, who had someone special they wanted to see again, others because they wanted freedom for all Berliners, contributing both money and time.

We worked in shifts day and night for several weeks with back-breaking effort, for the tunnel which began in the cellar twelve metres below ground could be no more than 70 centimetres high. According to our calculations, if we made it any bigger the rooms would be too small to take the soil and sand we were excavating.

Barrow load after barrow load it seemed to me, tired as I was from my weeks working on the assembly line at the factory. It would have been interesting to find out just how many barrows of dirt we removed, but no one kept a tally.

Not a bad mathematical problem for the schoolchildren, I mused.

‘If a barrow holds x amount of soil and sand, how many barrow loads would it take to empty an area 70 centimetres high x 145 metres long?’

I have learned since that it was the longest tunnel of its kind and also the most successful in terms of mass escapes from East to West.

On my shifts underground I felt I had an affinity with allied soldiers who dug their way out of the camps during the Second World War, the difference being that we were, at the time of construction, going into enemy territory, not trying to get out.

A scream from below brought me swiftly back to the present. The winch had caught leaving a claustrophobic teenage girl hanging helpless and terrified. It had happened many times while we were moving the pushcarts of dirt and was not difficult to rectify, but the screaming girl had to be silenced if she was not to give away the position to the guards at their command post not far from the eastern entrance. She, after all, was already in the west but there were many, like Karl, who would be much more vulnerable if they were alerted.

I inched towards her, hand over hand, down the cable, as I had done many times before, till I found the link which had caught, freed it with the ease of something well practised. Then, clasping a hand over her mouth, made a signal to Hans who, until that moment, had been standing behind me, that we were ready to come to the surface.

I was thankful when she was taken from me so I could resume my vigil, thankful too that people were still coming through, that her cries had not, after all, raised any kind of alarm.

Karl was the last man out that night. My brother, whose only crime in August 1961 had been that he was visiting a sick friend, sentenced to a life without his family because of Russian hatred for a past generation of my people.

We hugged, holding each other close for a long time, as if by letting go we would be separated again, crying unashamed tears into each other’s shoulders.

The next night, he and I stood side by side in the cellar of the Bernauer Strasse Bakery and helped to bring out twenty-nine more people. We made jokes about getting the whole of East Berlin through if we were lucky enough for the tunnel to remain undiscovered.

That, alas, was not to be, for the following day the wild animals did find their way into the cave and sealed its entrance forever.

Nothing Lasts Forever

Margaret Ward

Every Saturday morning Sally walked the half-mile trip to her grandmother's house. Her gran had lived in the same house all her life; it sat on its own at the end of a lane that would only take one car at a time. Neighbours were dotted around, but the area was very remote. The pace of living was slow, but the village was a very friendly place to live, everybody knew each other and helped when they could. The houses were made of stone with a lot of ground around each one, much of the ground was farmland and the owners either kept sheep or cattle. Sally's father was a farmer; they owned acres of ground and kept sheep, which were frequently taken to market. Since Sally's grandad had died about five years ago now, the garden at her gran's house had become very overgrown. It was too much for her gran to manage really, but she wouldn't move from her house.

Sally had been doing this same walk to her gran's house for nearly a year now. It had started after her gran had taken a fall and broken her hip. The fall had left her shaken and knocked her confidence, so she never left the house now. She relied on her stick all of the time, but as she was seventy-three now, Sally never minded running errands for her, or anyone else come to that. She liked to help whenever she could.

So, every Saturday morning, Sally set off for her gran's house with the groceries in a basket hanging on her arm. It was mostly downhill to her gran's house, which made it easier to carry the shopping, she was pleased that it wasn't uphill all the way. She never minded though as she loved her gran very much, their time together gave them the chance to talk and was very special.

Sally lived with her parents; she was an only child and very often had wondered what it would be like to have had brothers and sisters around. She was eleven years old, very bright, and Sally considered herself very grown up. Her father grew all different types of vegetables, he employed two men to help him on the farm but he was still kept very busy, especially in the lambing season.

Sally always helped her gran to put the shopping away. Afterwards they had tea and cake. They talked together about a lot of things, sometimes it was about the farm and sometimes about school. There were always cakes to eat that her gran had made and Sally took some home to her parents. Her gran had often told Sally how much she looked forward to Saturdays, that seeing her brought a ray of sunshine into the house every week.

It took Sally about half an hour to walk between the two houses. She always left in time to be home by three, which her mother wanted so as to be home before darkness fell. It was a glorious walk in the spring and summer, even the autumn was pretty, but the winter was a different story. It would soon be Christmas and the family would all be together again, as her gran was staying at Sally's house again this year.

As they were chatting together over a cup of tea, a car roared by outside at the end of the lane. Sally commented how fast and noisy it was.

'It keeps happening lately, Sally. They race down the lanes but it's got to be stopped, it's worse in the evenings though. Someone will be hurt soon if nothing is done about it,' her gran replied.

'It's spoiling the peace and quiet,' Sally answered. This was typical of Sally, liking to keep everything the same. She had always enjoyed the peacefulness of the countryside and had a love for animals and birds that lived in it.

As Sally got her coat on to return home, she was telling her gran about the carol singing that evening at the church hall.

'You have a lovely time, Sally, and I'll see you soon.'

Sally set off, thinking about the evening to come. Father Christmas was visiting at the church hall during the carol-singing. She was very eager to get home so she decided to run some of the way, until the hill became too steep, then she walked fast.

The wind was so bitterly cold against her face that it made her catch her breath. Sally huddled beneath her coat, trying to keep warm. She heard the cars' roaring engines and the brakes screeching on the bends of the lane. Gran was right, it was very noisy and dangerous. *Maybe the villagers could put a stop to it,* she thought to herself. When she got home she would tell her parents about it, and also that Gran needed another blanket to keep her warm now winter was here. Maybe we could get her one for Christmas.

It was now sleeting and with the wind and sleet blowing into her, Sally was having a job to see as she screwed her eyes up against it. She was deep in thought about the evening at the church and didn't hear the car behind her until it was too late …

Sally's mother was beginning to worry now. It had gone three and Sally hadn't arrived home. She told herself off for fussing, but knew that it was out of character for Sally to be late. If she didn't arrive soon she would ring her mother to see what time she'd left. It was no good, she couldn't settle. Something was wrong, she could feel it. She decided to call her mother and find out what was happening.

'She left at the normal time love, as she does every Saturday.'

'But she hasn't come home, Mum. I will walk and see if I can see her, if not I'm calling the police. I'll ring you back.' Replacing the receiver, she grabbed her coat and scarf. She would hold off calling her husband at the moment as he was at the market. It would be silly to worry him if there was nothing to worry about. Shutting the door behind her she made her way down the narrow path then out into the lane. As she walked and fought against the wind and sleet, she prayed so hard that her daughter would be all right. With a mobile phone in one hand and a torch in the other, she could feel her heart thumping against her ribs.

It was bitterly cold now and darkness was falling. All kinds of thoughts were racing through her mind. About halfway between her mother's house and hers she thought she heard a noise. It sounded like a whine. She stopped walking for a moment and listened again. No, it was gone. Maybe it was a cat or something. She proceeded to walk when she heard it again. It was a pitiful cry, very faint. It sounded like 'Help' but the wind was howling through the trees, making it very difficult to decipher. Waving her torch around, she suddenly spotted something on the grass verge. Hurrying along to it she felt the panic rise up inside of her. There, lying on the grass verge, was her daughter. 'Sally my darling, what happened? Goodness me, you're frozen.' She took off her coat, forgetting how cold it was, and laid it over her daughter.

Sally opened her eyes and then closed them again. Her mother noticed that her leg was buckled underneath her as she called the ambulance. Sally was drifting in and out of consciousness; her mother knew that all she could do was to try and keep her as warm as possible and to keep talking to her.

After what seemed like an eternity, the ambulance arrived. Sally's mother cried with relief. At the hospital she was assessed and then immediately taken to theatre. Her leg was broken in two places. She had internal injuries, concussion and hypothermia. Sally would be spending this Christmas in the hospital, but that didn't matter, what mattered was her daughter was alive. She said a silent prayer, thanking God for not taking their daughter away from them.

That evening at the hospital, the doctor spoke to Sally's parents. He explained that although the surgery was done, the next couple of days would be touch and go. Sally had suffered massive internal injuries and it was amazing that she was still alive. All they could do was to sit and wait.

Christmas Eve came and went, her family stayed with Sally all day at the hospital. She seemed to be making good progress. At least she was more awake now. On Christmas morning her mother wheeled her gran in to visit her. She had naturally blamed herself for the accident, and was very pleased to see her granddaughter was awake.

'When I'm better Gran, I'll visit you again on Saturdays.'

'There won't be any need for that Sally, because after Christmas I am coming to live with you permanently, so from now on there will be no more shopping trips up and down hills.'

'Oh Gran, that will be great. It will be lovely having you live with us all the time.'

Boxing day morning was very bright and sunny. The sleet that had fallen hadn't developed into snow. The house was relatively quiet after the hectic days at the hospital. The telephone ringing broke the peace.

'Mrs Hughes, can you get to the hospital as soon as possible please, Sally has taken a turn for the worse.'

The words ringing in her ears made her heart thump and miss a beat. On arriving at the hospital they were met by the doctor who had been looking after Sally. He ushered them into a small private room.

'What's happened? Can we see Sally?'

'I'm sorry but your daughter passed away five minutes ago. She suffered a massive heart attack very suddenly, her internal injuries were too much for her body to cope with. We did all we could but couldn't save her, I'm so sorry.'

The whole village mourned Sally's death. It was a lovely funeral, but life was never the same for the family. The person who drove into Sally and left her for dead was never found, but there was no more speed racing along the lanes.

Maybe Sally was now an angel, still helping and smiling at everyone she met. The one thing her mother did know was that Sally had been too good for this world. She cherished the eleven years that they'd had with her. Their own little angel had now returned back home.

Family Business

Anne Rolfe-Brooker

Victoria slammed the boot of her car shut and lowered the heavy shopping bags to the floor. She straightened up again to push her hair out of her face and wondered what on earth had possessed her to go food shopping on what forecasters were calling the hottest day of the year so far.

With a sigh she picked up the heavy bags and walked up the driveway to her front door. As she approached, she noticed the door to be ajar. With alarm, Victoria dropped the shopping bags where she was and ran inside. The downstairs of the house appeared just as she'd left it. With fear rising in her stomach she headed for the stairs. She checked the bedrooms and then moved towards the bathroom door. As she opened it, a gasp caught in her throat. She leant on the sink to steady herself, for there before her eyes in the bathtub, as large as life, and soaping himself as though he had no care in the world, was her dead uncle Gregory.

Now this august, and undoubtedly naked gentleman, had died when Victoria was quite small, and she therefore had no very real recollection of her mother's brother. The family, however, had often referred to him as a mean-souled, misanthropic miser, qualities which Victoria was certain she did not want in her bathtub, nor indeed anywhere else in her house.

Uncle Gregory looked at Victoria with the air of a startled pig (he had rather small beady eyes), and rather self-consciously covered his manhood with one hand. 'Good God, woman, don't you knock before you burst in upon other people's ablutions?' he enquired grumpily.

Surprise deserted Victoria and something akin to rage took over, although she was horribly aware that she was actually conversing with somebody who, by rights, had no business to be conversing with anyone except his Maker. 'What are you doing in my bathtub?' she demanded.

Uncle Gregory raised his eyes to Heaven, as though thoroughly unable to grasp the depths of stupidity to which his niece had descended. 'What do people generally do in bathtubs?' he asked testily. 'I am having a bath. Ten years in the soot and smoke of the lower regions don't exactly make for fragrant personal hygiene.'

Victoria stood for about fifteen seconds, motionless, while she mentally weighed up this last remark. 'Well, why don't you go back to where you came from, and leave my damned bathtub immediately?' she countered.

Uncle Gregory looked decidedly irate at this point, which is not an easy thing to do when found naked and uninvited in one's relative's bath, at the best of times. 'Do you think, Victoria, that we could continue this conversation in the living room in, say, ten minutes' time, as the water is getting rather cold and I do not wish to contract a chill.'

'I was not aware of the fact that one could contract anything once one had died,' his niece answered rather sniffily.

Uncle Gregory snorted, 'Indeed one can. I myself have just recovered from something rather unpleasant passed on by a succubus from the fourth layer of Hell, although,' he added, winking rather suggestively at Victoria, 'she was well worth the inconvenience!'

Victoria shuddered. 'Very well, I shall expect you downstairs, decently attired in ten minutes, Uncle Gregory, although I don't see any sign of discarded clothing in my bathroom.'

'Fear not, dear niece. One comes fully equipped on a working holiday, so if you would be so kind ...'

Victoria turned and walked down the stairs and into the living room, where she collapsed, somewhat numbed, onto the sofa. She sat for some moments, contemplating the utter lack of consideration the dead gentleman had shown in deciding to haunt her, and wondered for how long this ghostly visitation would last. The air in the room was somewhat humid and stuffy, Victoria having overlooked opening a window, understandably having other considerations on her mind, but she was pulled sharply out of her reverie by the sudden chill around her, occasioned by her deceased uncle entering the room. He was thankfully fully clothed, although the style was somewhat reminiscent of the 80s and he had a silver-topped walking cane in his left hand.

'Well,' he said pleasantly, 'I think we shall jolly along quite nicely, you and I, although personally,' he added, looking somewhat fiercely around the living room, 'I am not over-keen on lavender wallpaper.'

His niece stared at the apparition disbelievingly. Apart from the fact that she had spent some two months finding the precise shade of lavender about which he now seemed ultra critical, she had no intention of 'jollying along', at least not with a ghost, and such a thoroughly unpleasant ghost, judging by his behaviour so far. 'I am afraid that you are labouring under a misapprehension, Uncle Gregory. I do not require your presence, and whatever reasons you feel you have for haunting me …'

Her uncle waved his cane aloft, narrowly missing an expensive Meissen figurine which had pride of place on the cabinet next to him. 'My dear girl, one does not come from the lower layers on a mission of joy and peace. Indeed, the contrary is true. I have been sent on a working holiday to make your existence as miserable as possible. It is a requirement laid down by Management that every twenty years or so, the very worst of Hell's population has to visit a friend or relative to frighten the life out of them. It also helps deal with the over-population we are experiencing at the moment. But you, I see, are made of sterner stuff.'

'Well you can't stay here,' Victoria said sternly. 'I'm giving a dinner party this evening, and I can't have dead people running round scaring my guests.'

Uncle Gregory looked quite angry. 'For a start, I have no intention of running around. Such volatile behaviour would be most unseemly. And for another thing, I am afraid that I have nowhere else to go. You were the only one in the family who left the front door open, and in occult terms, this is considered an invitation, so in I popped, and a jolly cold reception I got, too!'

Victoria stood up and looked the old gentleman straight in his beady blue eyes. 'Well you can pop out now, the same way you popped in. If I inadvertently left the door ajar, it was certainly not as an invitation to any passing denizen of Hell, or indeed anyone else for that matter. Failing that, I shall call a priest and get you exorcised.'

Uncle Gregory looked decidedly uncomfortable. 'I don't think that would work,' he said with a degree of uncertainty and hesitancy in his voice. 'Although I must admit the thought of holy water does give me the shivers.'

'It's a shame the bath didn't have the same effect on you,' Victoria remarked, coldly. 'But you decidedly can't stay here, and that's final.'

The old man fumbled in his jacket pocket and brought out a large black handkerchief, with which he proceeded to dab at his eyes. 'But what is to be done?' he asked querulously. 'I can't go back without haunting you for at least a week. You'd be horrified at the punishments meted out to …'

Victoria raised a hand to silence him. 'Well, can you make yourself invisible, and be as quiet as a mouse when I have company?' she demanded.

The old man raised grateful if piggy eyes to her. 'Oh yes, I can do that,' he said. 'Only you will be able to see me, and I won't tip things over people or do the usual ill-bred haunting stuff. Just let me stay a week and I'll be off like a shot.'

Victoria smiled. 'Well, perhaps you could tip a little gravy, just a little, over Mr Clowers,' she said. 'He never did give me the raise he promised me ...'

My Dream

Mary Long

I first had the dream in the autumn of 1962, but my dreams are never quite dreams, they always start the same and I always want to wake, but the dream goes on.

I had not been well, I had a cold and my head ached, my throat was sore and my temperature was raging. It was the middle of October and the wind howled, the rain pelted onto the windowpanes and the sea roared its might as it hit land.

I went to bed, and it was just past midday, the dream began at once and I wanted to wake, I felt terror and sorrow. I was standing on a mountainside and the rain lashed at my face. I could see nothing, but the wind howled and echoed in the valley below, then I realised that the mountain was moving beneath my feet and I was awake.

I had never felt such terror and the sorrow was unbearable. I sat on the edge of the bed and looked at my watch. It was 12.05pm.

I was no stranger to dreams and I would always write them down on awakening, but this dream had terrified me and the emotion of sorrow weighed down on me. As the tears flowed down my face, I knew I was witness to something so horrible and devastating that the whole world would cry. I went downstairs and made a coffee and sat and thought, and still the tears fell from my face. There was horror there in the future, but how far in the future? I didn't know, I couldn't know.

Over the next few days I dreamed the dream every time I went to sleep. And then as Christmas approached the dreams stopped, and so Christmas came and went, and it was March when I again had the dream. The March winds were gale force and the sea thundered onto the shoreline, sending its spray inland. I looked out through the window and saw the sea crash over the pier walls and then swill its way back. I thought of my dream and what it meant and began to wonder where that mountain was.

It was that night I was to find myself again on that mountainside, with the twin emotions of terror and sorrow, but something was different, the mountain was moving at a faster pace and I was awake, the tears streaming from my eyes, and I was shaking with terror. From that night onward, that dream would reoccur many times.

In early October of 1966, the dream once more changed. I stood on the mountain to witness a grey dawn and the rain blew in my face and the wind howled in a melancholy way. The mountain now moved at speed and I was awake.

I ran to the bathroom shaking with fear and was sick with grief, I knew a tragedy of enormous proportion was about to happen and I had no way of averting the horror of what was to come. The days went by and I felt awful. My dream was there in my mind's eye all the while, and then as gale force winds tore their way through the Solway Firth, I went to bed, the date October 20th 1966. I stood on the mountain and looked into the valley, it was shrouded in mist. The rain fell and I believed them to be tears, the music was of a haunting kind, and I wanted to wake but the dream went on, a ray of sunlight so brilliant that it all but blinded me shot into the valley and I was awake.

Tragedy was about to strike, and it did on the 21st of October 1966, a mountain fell upon a school, and the little village of Aberfan died that day.

THE COURSE

Stephen Humphries

We never should have gone there, it was a waste of time and money, but Ivor was adamant, the company was failing and he thought we needed a boost. Something that would get us working like a well-oiled machine, I think were his exact words. Well, we were halfway there, if being well-oiled was the main requirement.

Ivor, our fearless leader and owner of our small company, was in a dilemma. He was the proud owner of a first-rate education and a second-rate business that was fast going down the tubes. Sales figures for the last quarter were off the chart, that is, somewhere in the basement. He thought this adventure weekend, aimed at building character and teamwork, was just what the firm needed. He'd seen it advertised in one of the better magazines and booked us in for three days of Hell. Well, he certainly brought the characters.

The drive down to the retreat should have been an enjoyable experience. As the longest serving, or as some said - longest suffering, employee, I got to sit up front with Ivor, who looked like he was born to be behind the wheel of his top of the range BMW. The other three members of our team squeezed into the rear seat. I did my best not to make eye contact with them in the mirror, but even so I could detect Tony's angry vibes.

I guess Tony was my soulmate in the firm, or at least my steady drinking partner. As Tony never married and I'd just come out of a messy divorce, we tended to have a lot of things in common, like sitting in bars for hours on end, and talking about a past that wasn't that great, even first time round. We were about the same age, the wrong side of forty, and Tony was a city boy, like me. He frowned now at the open green spaces that passed his window, an alien landscape to all of us. He might have benefited from the fresh air had Trish, our below average receptionist, not lit up a cigarette, her fourth since we started the journey. Her excuse that it made her eat less was defeated by the two Mars bar wrappers at her feet.

Trish was a big woman, with big appetites, as she kept hinting to Scott, our fifth and last member of the group. Trish was married to a little man with a big house, and she neglected both. She now jammed her ample thigh against young Scott, who sat crouched in the corner with both hands over his crotch, counting passing sheep and praying for sleep.

'Tom, lower that window a bit, will ya, I'm dyin' back here,' Tony said from behind me.

I fiddled with the array of knobs and buttons at my side, looking for the right one. Ivor pushed something on his side and a blast of cold, crisp air assaulted me.

'Teamwork!' Ivor shouted, chuckling like a maniac on his way to a hanging, the grin of a zealot upon his face.

I forced a smile and checked my seatbelt for the umpteenth time. It was going to be a long weekend.

The converted farmhouse that was to be our home for the next three days had an air of sadness about it, a desolate house in a desolate place. Terry, our instructor for the course, stood at the door in welcome, an insincere smile plastered to his face. I immediately thought of a second-hand car salesman, and the way he gave the BMW the once over only confirmed his previous profession. We were ushered in to meet his partner, Dickie, though whether this was a business or domestic relationship we weren't told, and even now, I'm not sure. Looking back, I got the impression that Terry didn't let a little thing like gender get in the way of having a good time.

We signed the book and were allotted our rooms. Tony insisted on sharing with me, which I found endearing, until he confessed his hatred for the rest of the team. Young Scott stuck close to Ivor, the prospect of sharing with Trish just too much to bear. However, Ivor pulled rank and bunked alone, leaving Scott to the mercy of our wanton receptionist. Counting sheep would be the least of his worries.

We retired to our rooms to freshen up and resurfaced that evening to a nice meal laid on by Dickie, whose culinary skills might just save the weekend. The after-dinner drinks reverted into a booze-up where Tony and I swapped war stories at the bar, while Trish tried to get to grips with Scott. Terry hovered in the background, giving both Trish and Scott the eye, while Ivor practised his manic grin in the mirror.

Next morning we surfaced, hangovers and regret the order of the day. Trish popped down to tell us Scott was running a bit of a fever, but she would nurse him back to health. She helped herself to two breakfasts and a bottle of wine and hurried back upstairs, hips swaying provocatively. Poor Scott was about to experience the effects country air had on a healthy woman. The rest of us made do with a manly fry-up while we listened to Terry outline our day. We were to take a brisk bicycle ride through the nearby foothills, following a map with cryptic clues, to our final destination, where, we were informed, a worthy prize awaited us. His idea to split us into two groups was defeated somewhat by our depleted numbers but he gamely agreed to accompany Ivor when, once again, Tony insisted on staying with me, casting some doubt on our own relationship!

I hadn't been on a bicycle since I left school and soon felt my age. Tony and I cycled at a leisurely pace, after Tony spat up what appeared to be half a lung that may or may not have contained bones! It seemed we were both new to the great outdoors. The other team had raced off in the opposite direction, wheel matching wheel and smarmy grin matching smarmy grin. Ivor was taking things way too serious and the contest soon descended into one of those macho things that nobody was prepared to lose. Tony, on the other hand, felt no further need of the map once we came upon the nearest village, and more importantly, the nearest village pub. He tossed the map over his shoulder and his bike found the nearest ditch. I dropped my bicycle onto his.

'Should we lock them?' I asked, reverting back to my Dublin mind-set.

'Naw, with a bit of luck someone will have them away,' he said, and strode manfully into the bar, to discover if the natives were friendly.

After our fourth pint we tucked into the sandwiches which Dickie had thoughtfully packed for us.

'A good man, that Dickie,' Tony said between mouthfuls.

High praise indeed from someone who had issues with humanity.

The day flew in and the natives did indeed prove to be friendly. My visa card was put through its paces and it would take some creative accounting to bill this down to company expenses. We arrived back to the farmhouse as the sun went down, two bicycles sticking out of the boot of the local taxi. Ivor and Terry had beaten us by some hours and the strain on Ivor's face told me that the prize, a voucher offering 50% discount on our next visit, was not an option we were likely to exercise.

Once again, Dickie saved the day with a slap-up meal, before we retired to our rooms for a power-nap.

That evening, we all piled into Terry's Transit van for our visit to the local village. Dickie dispensed with his apron and proved he knew his way around a gin bottle. Trish and Scott declined to come, though Trish assured us Scott was making huge improvements. Tony and I were welcomed like long-lost sons in the bar and this time Ivor's credit card took the strain. Poor Ivor, it was obvious that things weren't working out as he'd hoped and he'd taken to grinding his teeth, a nasty habit that lasted long after the trip was finished. Tony, on the other hand, was having a ball. A city dweller all of his life, gone were the hard lines and negative frown, and he was even heard to inquire about property prices towards the end of the night. Ivor and Terry propped up the bar and patched up their differences. Unable to resist, Terry even made an offer for the BMW, which was politely declined.

Sunday, our final day, dawned bright, but none of us were up to see it. We struggled out mid-morning, like survivors of some natural disaster. We made do with strong coffee, as Dickie was still wrestling with the gin bottle, which explained why a chef of his calibre hid his light under such a rural bushel. Trish and Scott still hadn't surfaced, but if the noise from their room was anything to go by, it sounded like Scott had got his strength back. Terry was on hand, smile in place and itinerary tucked under his arm. Maybe it was the body language, or maybe just the hangovers, but he didn't push the orientation exercise he had planned, and settled for a leisurely stroll around the local lanes before we departed for the long drive home.

I swapped seats with Tony for the return trip. He said he wanted to view the *For Sale* signs as we passed and who was I to argue? I squeezed in beside the lovebirds in the back. Scott looked terrible. He had dark circles under his eyes and he might have lost weight. His pale skin looked even paler, and he had a look of horror in his eyes usually reserved for war correspondents. Trish, on the other hand, looked great, and the Mars bar, packet of crisps and twenty smokes in her lap showed she'd lost none of her appetites. She held Scott's hand as he stared out the window. He didn't notice the sheep anymore.

We stopped about halfway home at a filling station, where we topped up with petrol and some fast food. Dickie's culinary delights were already a fading memory. We sat munching our burgers and chips on cheap plastic seats in a cheap plastic restaurant.

'Have you learned anything?' Ivor asked us, scanning our faces.

Scott had the decency to blush. Trish munched her Big Mac, an inscrutable look upon her face. Tony looked almost healthy, a rosy glow to his cheeks, though that could have been last night's whisky.

'I've got to get out of 'the Smoke' more often,' he said and nodded his head.

I diplomatically remained silent; I'd already known how to get drunk.

I offered to drive the rest of the way but Ivor declined. He seemed to be getting back to his old self. As a bonding exercise the weekend was a non-starter, with the possible exception of Trish and Scott. He would have to find some other ways to motivate his team. He gnashed his teeth and wondered if mountaineering was the answer?

As we drew closer to the city, reality raised its ugly head. Trish released Scott's hand and lit another cigarette, reflecting on the hopeless staying power of today's youth. Scott placed his own hands back over his crotch, a case of closing the stable door after the horse has bolted. Tony found his frown long before we found the smog. I flicked through the Sunday papers we'd picked up at the gas station.

'Checkin' the football results, are ya?' asked Ivor through the rear view mirror.

I smiled and nodded my head. I didn't have the heart to tell him I was looking at the 'Situations Vacant' column. Oh well.

A Doctor's Dilemma
Lynda S Heaton

Brenda Richards was taking an overdue and well-earned break from the surgery where she was one of four doctors. They had been one doctor short on the duty rota now for a number of months, and the workload of each had increased greatly, putting them all under tremendous pressure. It was now her turn to have a holiday and she had decided that her lounge was in dire need of redecoration. The preparation done and paint bought, she could now, whenever she chose, wield the paintbrush.

She was standing at her front garden gate dressed in her 'painting togs'; dark green dungarees and a pair of well-worn trainers.

'Armed and dangerous, eh Doc?' smiled Fred Renshaw, nodding towards the paintbrush still clasped in her hand, the bristles covered in lavender-coloured paint. He was her next-door neighbour and also stood at his gate.

'Mmm? Oh yes,' she replied, her mind preoccupied, looking towards the forest opposite their homes. Had she taken more notice of Fred, she would have seen he looked a little strange, not the usual Fred.

It was the commotion at the forest edge that had bought her out into the autumn evening air. Dusk had fallen and the air was becoming a little chilly. Brenda shivered but her curiosity aroused, she intended to stay there for a little longer. A police helicopter circled above and a line of police officers had assembled along the outer edge of the forest. At a shouted command, the officers moved slowly forward into the forest.

Vans of different shapes, colours and logos started to arrive, parking wherever space allowed along the grass verge. People emerged from the rear of these vehicles, carrying microphones, cameras and lighting equipment. Brenda watched this frenzy of bodies jostling and squabbling for what they believed to be the best vantage point for whatever news was to be gathered. As she stood observing the melee, from the corner of her eye she saw a police officer approaching.

'Doctor Richards? I'm Inspector Burrows.' He held out his hand.

'Inspector.' She shook his hand. She thought he looked familiar, but just couldn't place where she had seen him before. He unnerved her too, but she didn't know why.

'We have a bit of a situation, and your help would be appreciated, if you wouldn't mind?' His eyes never leaving hers as he spoke.

'If I can,' she replied, her eyes drawn to his and no matter how hard she tried, she could not look away. As an unfounded panic started to seize her, he looked away, breaking the invisible hold.

'We could do with a bit of medical help,' he said and gestured with his hand towards the forest. 'I'll escort you now if you don't mind.'

This was said not as a question, but a command. Brenda replied she would change and get her medical case, but the inspector insisted she was fine as she was, he would get another officer to pick up her bag, and grabbed her firmly by the elbow and escorted her across the road.

It was getting dark and as she looked into the forest there was nobody to be seen. She thought the police officers must now be deep inside, but it had looked as though they were going to do a thorough search, so it struck her as odd that they had gone so far so fast.

'Okay Doctor. If you would just walk straight ahead through the trees, another officer will meet you.' With that the inspector turned and walked towards the crowd of reporters.

As Brenda left the tree edge, what little of the light that was left started to fade. She walked faster, hoping to see a police figure emerge from the gloom, as much to calm her rising panic as to know she would soon be near the place she was needed. The trees loomed tall and thick all around her and seemed to take on a menacing quality. She could hardly see five yards ahead, it had gone quite dark and a mist had started to swirl around, wispy at times, quite thick at others. Not a sound emerged from the forest, only her laboured breath as she broke into a run, dodging branches that reached out to entangle her hair and clothes; tree roots breaking the surface she ran over, trying to trip her every step. She had no idea in which direction she had been running, trying to keep in a straight line, and hoped she was still heading in the right direction. Out of breath, Brenda came to a halt, leant against the nearest tree and, gasping for air, slowly looked around. What she saw terrified her.

Gone was the living forest, to be replaced by dead old gnarled tree trunks. She could see glowing pinpoints of yellow and orange surrounding her, varying in height, and instinctively knew they were the eyes of something threatening, but couldn't make out the shapes behind them.

She called out, hoping to hear a reply from the officer that was supposed to be meeting her, but after the echo of her voice died away, silence was the only reply. She could hear shuffling movements combined with a sort of grunting, growling sound and she turned in terror and fled. She ran in blind panic, stumbling, lurching, regaining her balance again and again, and all the time she could hear the chasing hordes of goodness knew what, right behind her. She ran until she could run no more, staggering to a standstill. The noise behind her also stopped. She looked around frantically trying to find refuge; finding none she turned and stood with her back against the large tree to face whatever it was that was chasing her. Looking down at her hand, she was amazed to find she still held the paintbrush.

A weapon, she thought triumphantly. The tree trunk she had backed against suddenly became soft and she could feel herself being drawn into it. She tried to struggle free but her arms were trapped. She tried to scream but no sound emerged from her throat. As she fought to free herself she could see the slits of those many evil glowing eyes getting closer.

Brenda suddenly awoke from her nightmare, wrestling with the duvet that had, in her restless sleep, enveloped her. With her heart beating quickly and heavily in her chest she freed herself, then lay for a few moments until she was calm. Suddenly her doorbell rang, startling her. Quickly getting out of bed and into her dressing gown she descended the stairs to the front door. Opening the door, her heart missed a beat, there on her doorstep stood a police officer.

'Doctor Richards?' he enquired.

She swallowed the panic rising in her throat and replied, 'Yes officer, can I help you?'

'We're sorry to inconvenience you, but we have an incident down at the station and wondered if you could attend, as Doctor Weatherspoon isn't available?'

Relief washed over Brenda and she smiled inwardly. Replying she would attend given ten minutes to get ready, the officer nodded, turned and walked back to the waiting police car.

COSTEL'S DAY

Mariana Zavati Gardner

Costel got up in the morning at the sound of the bright cockerel. It was perched on the shed of the people living next door. He felt a warm buzz going up and down his average-sized body. He was well-built due to those never-ending drills from his days spent at the military academy. Such a long time ago!

The heat was already touching the room opening into a long balcony, shadowing the neighbours' house, like a blessing. He got out of bed, went to the bathroom and got himself ready for the day ahead.

In the compact kitchen, the old tabby cat was asleep, twitching now and then. Costel's daughter was already up for a last minute revision for that week's language oral exams. The milk was already hot for the morning café au lait, the bread was rather hard and on the way to turning stale.

'Good morning, Mariana. Have you slept well?' he asked his daughter. Her reply came after a sip of coffee.

'Not really, as I had to go to bed after midnight. I still had so much to revise for today's French oral. I don't know if I can remember anything of what the teacher had taught me. I tell you she hasn't got too much knowledge of French herself.'

'Now, now, I shall have no bad words said about my colleagues. Such a committed teacher,' her father replied. Costel would never get involved in any argument. He would never take sides, though deep down he was a person of very strong personal opinions. However, he liked to keep his thoughts to himself.

'Who knows nothing of the subject after all,' the young lady replied frustrated. She could feel her temper building up and that might not have been a good omen before such a bothering exam. She was turning the pages of her revision exercise book like a fashion magazine, without taking anything in.

'Mother is coming home from Bucuresti today and Grandma will see about lunch for you. What time is your exam?' he asked her rather distracted. He sipped from his coffee and looked thoughtful.

'About eleven. I feel so bad about it,' she went on.

'I wouldn't if I were you. You have already been to France and Paris and you are rather fluent in the language,' he encouraged her. He took a piece of bread and dipped it in his coffee. Costel was a frugal eater.

'But I don't know enough vocabulary and possibly not enough of the horrid irregular verbs,' she replied rather upset now.

'Look, I have tested you last night and your grandma has checked some of the irregular verbs. All in all you know enough for this exam. Look, I need to leave for school now as my first candidate is due in half an hour. Good luck! Look on the bright side! You'll amaze them all with your knowledge,' he ended, putting his plate and cup in the deep kitchen sink.

Costel closed the kitchen door behind him and went into the hall and out of the apartment locking the door behind him. He went down the one flight of steps to the ground floor. The morning sun was bathing the plants at the entrance. There was a fragrance in the air of market produce and of fresh growing plants. Down the path, he closed the metal gate and went into the always quiet street, with very high poplars and broken pavement. He was proud of the poplars. He had planted them, with his own hands, years ago, after the first people had moved in. It was the 'in thing' to live in an apartment with all the mod cons.

He left the station market on his right. Farmers were early, with half of the produce already sold. The market was on the place of the new house built by the Munteanu's. It blew up shortly after being built due to a gas leakage. Both had died in horrendous pain in hospital. Luci, their married daughter, was living away at the time. Though she was not on speaking terms when her parents died, Luci gave them a much remembered funeral.

Costel passed the market and the empty land where a house had collapsed during a recent earthquake, without injuring a soul. He went till the end of the street, crossed the street and passed the old hotel which had been turned into a pub. In the old days, during the ancient regime, which one would mention only in a whisper, Ion, Costel's retired father-in-law, used to supply the vegetables for the restaurant of the hotel, which, at the time, had the best chef in town. This was the local for Mr Voicu Ichim, the best Romanian teacher in town, who, before lessons, used to come here for warmth and encouragement. The present pub was in close proximity of Costel's childhood bungalow. It looked neglected. It was so complicated to find any building material nowadays.

Costel went passed the row of houses in the street where his college was situated. Gardens were looking at their best and the fragrance was overwhelming. He left the open summer theatre on his right and reached the college in good time.

The college was a mighty building built with public money from public donations. It had been the inspiration of Mrs Ghervescu, who had been a spinster for a very long time until Colonel Ghervescu, who was getting on and whose eyesight was not as sharp as usual, proposed to her one day in circumstances unknown. From that day onwards he became a 'jack of all trades'.

Anyway, Costel opened the huge teachers' door and entered the school hall to be greeted by his chemistry colleagues.

The various Baccalauréat orals in many subjects were starting that day. Costel went upstairs on the grand staircase designed to frighten the younger and the older pupils alike. He entered the chemistry laboratory and went across the teachers' office where he had placed the oral questions which he had done some time before. The questions had been placed before in an old safe acquired by the old administration of the high-school during the ancient regime.

In those days they built things sturdy and to last, he thought. He knew that those were thoughts one could have to oneself, privately, when one went for a walk. Those were thoughts one was strongly advised never to utter in public. There were things one was supposed to believe in, but Costel was one of those who did not. He knew there was another side to things and he was able to remember good chunks of this from his younger years. All those years spent at the best military school in Cernovitz followed by the military academy in Wuppertal had shaped up his personality. His studies in chemistry at the University of Iasc that followed made him the best teacher in the region. However, he was continuously restless, often touched by a profound disillusion.

Miss Lipan, the lab assistant came in with the coffee. 'Good morning Sir! I asked your first candidates to get ready for the oral. I hope it's OK with you, Sir,' she said. Then she started dividing some materials and cataloguing them. It was a tedious job. Besides, she had to type a number of papers for the school's secretariat because none of the people in the office could type. She was friendly with Costel for he would translate her letters to her then German boyfriend. The relationship was frowned upon by the officials of the day glue stuck to their chairs of power. Due to the official climate, Miss Lipan's father in particular was obliged to disapprove of the relationship outside the house.

The regime was not encouraging meetings, encounters or relationships with foreigners. There were laws that were not allowing foreigners to be accommodated in private homes. Any private encounter had to be reported to the Securitate in writing. Interviews might possibly follow. Costel was visualising the security officers surrounded by a mountain of files. People did not dare show descent. Even jokes expressed in private were not safe. There were informers everywhere. They were employed to watch and find out the vibes of the people.

A thought passed Costel's mind about the 24 hours he had to spend at Securitate headquarters. At the time the authorities thought of him to be a western spy. This was because he had set the foundation of Radio Club of the county with a number of enthusiastic friends. They elected him as its first president. Costel's moments had been bright for a snippet. He had been able to be in contact with people from all over the world. This however ended very quickly. The authorities were making rules as they went on. He had been summoned at the Securitate headquarters shortly after midnight. Costel feared for his life as he had just finished listening to the illegal Voice of America radio program. He was taken by two agents. He had been left in an office on his own for 24 hours. Then someone in charge came back and sent him home. Costel was anxious to open any thought regarding his matter.

The morning went very quickly. He hardly had the time to spare a thought besides the exams.

Costel evaluated the morning exam in his mind. *It went well,* he thought. His pupils were always diligent. Besides, everybody knew of him. He must have taught half of the parents and the existing pupils in the town and in the adjacent localities. The high school was a boarding school, one of the elite high schools in the country, where delegations from abroad were brought in there to see and admire. Costel believed in his teaching and in this school of learning.

Costel put his papers aside and closed the oak door. He left the staff room behind, engulfed in silence and smell of polish. Maricica, the cleaner, had done an excellent job. The smell of beeswax on the walnut and oak bookcases, on the round and square tables was making them shine in the powerful afternoon sun.

Costel went to the Secretariat to see if there was anyone left there to exchange some thoughts about the day. There was no one in sight.

Costel made his way home, this time through the park because it was cooler. He then walked the street parallel with the railway warehouses, by Mr Lebegioara's who was his tailor of many years, then by Mr Berdescu the shoemaker; he passed the new cinema, an architectural achievement of the new regime. *A pity,* he thought, *that all the films were Russian war films. Terribly boring and badly made!* He stopped to see if he was able to buy something from any of the shops that were strung in front of the railway station, it had been built in the last century on the model of an English station; it had fresh hanging baskets ready to blast their fragrance in the cool of the evening after the usual afternoon rain.

There was nothing to buy. The shelves were empty again. Costel was not surprised at all. He was always carrying cash so he could be able to buy no matter what, even if the item was not necessarily immediately needed. It had become a habit for everybody to have some money just in case something turned up unexpectedly. This was established since the end of the 40s, after the new puppet regime, directed by the Kremlin rulers, took a strong and fearful grip on everything Romanian. Its tentacles were holding tight in people's minds. Costel had these thoughts all to himself. They were never to come out of his head. There were informers everywhere or one was meant to believe. They were present amongst pupils, who were the young 'pioneers', amongst all walks of life and amongst those of pensionable age.

They were recruited from those who had 'nothing to offer', but had good hearing and basic writing skills. Costel's downstairs neighbour was one of them. She would sit at the kitchen window hours on end, monitoring who was coming in and who was leaving. It was definitely a very trying endeavour. It required commitment and acute curiosity.

Costel got home. He found Mariana shining. 'I got maximum mark and congratulations from the examiner!' she said full of herself. That was indeed an achievement as she had decided to do this exam only a year ago. Iulia, her mother who strongly believed in private tuition like in the old days from before the war, went with her to Professor Ion Grigoriu. He found that Mariana, though she could speak French fluently, did not know any literature or grammar. Straightaway, the

Professor had sent her to two former pupils of his, the Pavel husband and wife who lived in Iasi, two hours drive from Bacau. They were both lecturers at the University there. They found her too far behind in that matter. Mariana's mother, the pharmacist, was immediately sent to another capable lecturer, Miss Petruta Spanu, who believed she could fill in the gaps as she grasped some 'form of linguistic talent'. Mariana was a dreamer inclined to study only what appealed to her. She had an agenda all of her own. Costel knew that very well.

While Costel was changing his summer suit, there was a knock at the door.

'Mariana, answer the door please. See who it is. If it's for your mother, say she'll be back from Bucuresti late tonight.'

Mariana answered the door. Mr Botez, her grandmother's neighbour was at the door. 'Good afternoon. Is your father at home?'

Mariana invited Mr Botez in. He was unusually tall and slender. He was the husband of Mariana's chemistry teacher. Mariana felt uneasy. She was not particularly fond of her teacher as she believed that this particular teacher disliked her. Costel came from the balcony.

'Good afternoon. How are you?' Mr Botez rubbed his hands. He clamped his feet.

He opened his mouth and the words came out, dry, stumbling. 'Costel, your mother has been taken ill. She has collapsed in the bathroom. She has hit her head. On the radiator. Hard. You know these iron cast ones.' Then he stopped.

Costel's lower lip was trembling. He turned towards Mr Botez and said like he used to say in his former army days, 'Let's go now!'

The Delivery Skipper

Don Tong

I lay wedged inside the coffin-sized box with the top inches above my face as it fills, the water sloshing over my chest and the stench of wood and sea water; my fear is overpowering. The cocaine doesn't matter now. A week ago it had all been so different.

I had just got back into port after a special delivery for Jack Johnson, Jenny's husband. We had agreed payment would be through the Port Captain and as soon as I had the boat secured I headed there. I picked up my cheque, but there was a message waiting for me as well. It was in Jack's unmistakably blunt wording.

'Stop out at the house, something important to discuss, cash no object.'

The taxi turned into a wide boulevard in Fort Lauderdale's millionaire row. Above us the noonday sun glared down rocketing the temperature in the car to over a hundred. Through high security gates, down sweeping drives, and between curtains of palm and evergreen trees I caught a sniff of real wealth. At Jack's place, we were passing through security and the driver pulled up in front of a mansion with white colonnades. I found the man in his study. At five-foot five, 280 pounds and wrapped in a loud Hawaiian shirt, he looked like a gift wrapped beach ball. He tilted his bald head up and glared at me.

'You're late, time is money. You ought to know that.'

I only half listened to the breathy remarks as I took in the room. The walls were lined with books in front of which were two Mediterranean style leather chairs. Like Jack, they looked hot and heavy. The only reprieve was a pungent sea breeze that gusted in through a set of French doors. Beyond them I could see a terrace, a good stretch of manicured lawn and in the distance a sailboat swung on her anchor.

'Nice yacht,' I said finally. 'Seventy footer more or less?'

'More or less, I got it for my wife, can't stand the God damn things myself but there you go. That's the business; I need someone to skipper it. You interested?'

I wasn't. My yacht, The Mistral and I had an agreement. She kept me safe and I was doing everything I could to get us to the Caribbean for the fall charter season. The deliveries I made for the man in front of me were a quick way to make money. All short jobs with the understanding I could leave when I wanted. The last thing on my list was to be stuck in a routine. I told Jack as much.

'We all got plans,' he said interrupting me. 'Plans were made to be broken. This is a business proposition and you know I pay well.'

'It isn't the money.'

Jack shifted his bulk back in his chair, one tree stump of a leg craned up and over the other. A look of incomprehension swept over his face. 'Bullshit. It's always about money.'

I wasn't interested but that wasn't going to wash with Jack. He had the power to have my boat locked up or worse. I had heard tales of people who had said no and ended up face down in the swamp. It was then that the door opened and Jenny came in.

'Is this him?' she said taking me in with a smile.

'Yeah,' Jack said.

By the look of the white shorts and top she had just come in from playing tennis. I don't know what kind of woman I expected Jack would marry, but somehow she didn't fit the bill. Her damp hair was cut short clinging to a round, heavy face. Intelligent eyes barely hid, I sensed even then, some deeper concerns. But the smile was warm, welcoming even. Gauging by the roll of fat around her waist she was way behind on her exercise schedule; it explained the tennis.

'Have you told him?' she said.

'Not everything. But I will now.' Jack heaved himself forward until his gut surged over the edge of the desk.

'Job's simple, Skipper. You'll be available. If Jenny says she wants to do some sailing at 6am, you'll take her out; noon, afternoon, after dark, all the same.'

And that was that.

A couple of hours later I had moved aboard. The boat was brand new with all the gear you would expect. I was about to start down into the engine room to familiarise myself with the ship's systems when I heard Jenny call my name.

I turned as she entered the gallery.

'You made it,' she said glancing around and then, 'you drink on duty?'

Before I could answer she was fishing beers out of the yacht's small fridge. She placed them, glasses and an opener on the gallery table before sitting down herself.

‘I wanted to talk to you,’ she said pouring out the drinks. She raised her glass, made an attempt at a smile and failed. ‘I need help.’

‘You’ll get the hang of sailing,’ I said, ‘I have taught …’

‘No, you don’t understand.’ She then hesitated a moment before continuing as if she wasn’t sure she should confide in me. ‘It’s to do with my husband …’

‘Whoa, I’m sorry,’ I said interrupting, ‘thanks all the same but that isn’t my problem. If you want to get the handle on setting sails fine. Radar navigation, I’m your man, but Jack is a big guy and he can do some damage …’

Jenny touched my arm. ‘No, wait until I explain something.’

She gave me a brief history of her marriage. She had been caught up in the back draught of a man that had pushed her out of his life. There had been a string of other women, incidents that had left her embarrassed and angry. He had given her the boat as a diversion; something that would occupy her and ease his conscience. When she finished she had one more revelation. ‘I want you to get me out of here.’

I looked at her and laughed. I couldn’t help it.

‘I have a boat in the marina,’ I explained. ‘A boat I want to get back aboard one day and sail away.’

‘If I told you, you would be able to afford any boat you wanted with more money then you could spend, would you at least hear me out?’

I sipped the beer, my mind wondering off to explore the idea. I had had my chance when my father offered me the family business. He had promised a salary of six figures and one day the big house would be mine. It wasn’t enough. I wanted the money all right, just not the tedium that went with it. What Jenny did next assured me that wouldn’t be a problem.

‘Come here a moment,’ she said and moved to the engine room hatch, pulled it back and descended the ladder. There wedged in a corner was a three-foot by seven-foot box. Jenny bent down and pried the lid off. Inside, across the bottom in even rows was bag after bag of what looked like white powder. She lifted one up awkwardly, held it away from her body as if it might be contaminated.

‘This is powdered gold. I hate it, hate what it does but when it comes down to it, I am saving myself.’

I felt a small, involuntary rush of air escape my lips.

'What are *you* doing with it?'

'Let's go up to the gallery,' Jenny said lowering the bag back into the box. In the boat's kitchen I chased up more beer while the woman continued her story.

'I suppose you wonder why I don't just file for a divorce and take what the court would award me. For one thing, Jack will never pay me a cent. He'll just get rid of me. This way is better. When he has to explain the loss to the people who count, they won't be pleased. Don't look so funny, I am only getting him before he gets me.'

I still didn't understand.

'How do you know anything about his business? For someone who is being pushed out of her husband's life ...'

'We weren't always this way. When the house was built Jack had a room put in below the main floor. I have always known about it and what he uses it for. When drugs come in from the Caribbean they are stored there until the market is right.'

I looked at her a moment and weighed up the odds. 'Suppose I agree, what's next?'

'Get the boat stocked up with a couple of month's supplies and whatever charts we will need for the Caribbean. I'll tell you when it is time.'

I watched her pick her way down the swim ladder. Just before stepping into the dingy she glanced back at me.

'I am, of course, presuming you want to go to the Caribbean.' When I didn't respond she continued, 'Smile Skipper, and think of it as just another delivery.'

Later that night I tried to sort out my options. I could get the hell out of there; down to the marina, on my boat and on my way south. But there was no way I would even clear the port entrance without Jack getting wind of it. Then there was the money but beyond that was the thrill of a great adventure. If Jenny came true, I wasn't going to be charting again.

By the end of the week the yacht was restocked. I took her to the fuelling quay, and then made sure the emergency equipment was up to scratch before picking up the charts we would need.

Later, back at the anchorage, Jenny turned up. 'Do you suppose we can sail tonight?'

'Sure ... guess so. What's going to stop Jack stopping us?'

Jenny smiled sweetly up at me. 'There is a tennis competition being staged in Bermuda and I'm scheduled to play. It's a week long affair, I told my husband it might be a good idea if we took the boat over on her maiden voyage. Jack couldn't keep the smile off his face knowing I would be out of his life for seven days. He is even throwing a going away party which I think is rather ironic under the circumstances. I want to leave after that.'

I watched as she headed back to shore.

That evening by seven the party was in full swing. The sky was heavy with massed storm clouds while below it, the lawn was ablaze in coloured lights. A large marquee had been erected; people were milling about and the faint sound of their voices drifted out to me across the choppy sea. I eventually went into the engine room and I was no sooner below when there was a the sound of gunfire. I raced back up to the bridge, grabbed a pair of field glasses and trained them on the house. The lawn had emptied. I searched the coast as heavy drops of rain began to spot the yacht's deck. There was what looked like a dingy moving away from the shore at high speed. Something was up and I got below and started moving bags up on deck. By the time Jenny pulled alongside, I had the box out as well.

'It's all coming apart,' she said breathlessly, clambering on-board.

'What happened?'

'Cubans - guns - they just started shooting. Let's go - get going.'

I checked the coastline one more time and caught sight of another boat leaving. 'There's no time,' I yelled. 'Help me get the box over the side.'

We hauled the container over to the ship's rail and lowered it down into the sea. I got in and as Jenny handed down the bags of cocaine, I spread them out as best I could.

'Lay down and I'll fit the top.' Jenny's voice was low and urgent.

'What ... ?'

'Get down, if they see you ...' Her voice was lost behind the barrier of wood sliding into place. This was followed by a loud hammering close to my head and I realised she was nailing me in. I choked back the panic and concentrated on the distraction of a small outboard engine's sputter that was coming out of the background. It grew louder, revved up high, as panicky as I was. The noise was about to run over the top of me when it suddenly died. Feet shuffled and scraped somewhere on the yacht's deck. I heard muffled talking - drifting in rhythm and tenor, fading, regaining strength and then nothing. *Can they be looking down wondering what a half submerged wooden container is doing alongside?* For some unfathomable reason I actually thought they were going to pull me out - that they would lift the top.

The feet shuffled again, the engine I heard before burst into life, shrieking at being called to duty, then slowly fading taking any hope away; lost in the slurp of sea wash inches from my face - a sea wash that surged and banged my small world against the yacht but the rocking was comforting somehow and the box was more like a cradle than a coffin. There were slivers of air coming in with cool fingers of water. The box was filling - not long now - hopeless - hope? What the hell was hope? There was no such thing - all gone and the panic faded to resignation. The cocaine didn't matter, the money wasn't important either, the reasons why any of it happened were slowly drifting away.

Then the box dipped hard and my body and the bags slid over. The nails screeched, the top was off and rain was splashing on my face. Above me Jenny was smiling and extending her hand.

'Get up, come on. You're going to drown in there,' she said helping me up on deck.

I watched her heave the wet bags onto the yacht. Later after a quick shower we motored slowly toward the harbour entrance and Jenny explained what had happened.

'They must have found out about the missing drugs. I just kept my head down and got into the boat as quickly as I could. The Cubans must have seen me and decided I was up to something. Thank God we got the stuff off the boat because when they searched they found nothing and left.'

'You nailed the lid down!'

'If they looked they wouldn't see anything. They weren't going to hang around long enough to lift the top.'

'What about the cocaine? Did water get into it?'

'No, the bags are waterproof.'

By dawn we were well out to sea. I rigged the sails and set our course south, south-east to pass a hundred miles off of Key West, Florida. Off to my left the sun was a red ball rising over the rolling sea. I wondered absently if it was somehow a warning. Still, if all went well, in a couple of days we would never be found. I knew where I could sell the boat. I didn't know if Jack had survived but I wasn't taking any chances. Besides, I liked the idea of something bigger with a longer range, a yacht that would cruise the world. It wouldn't be cheap, of course, but since when was money a problem?

Why Is She Here?

Patricia Smith

If you wanted to be kind you could say that the station buffet had an air of faded grandeur or perhaps a lived-in look. In fact, it was scruffy; if you looked closely you could see the grime on the tables, the bits of peeling wallpaper and the cracks in the plaster. Jane saw none of these. Although the room had been empty when she came in, and still was, she had chosen the table in the corner, at the back, squeezing herself into the smallest possible space. She was used to that; it was the way she had lived her life; trying not to get noticed.

If you wanted to be kind you could say that Jane's clothes were shabby chic or had a bohemian air. In fact, she too was scruffy; if you looked closely you might conclude that Oxfam was her shop of choice. But there you would be wrong. Jane bought her clothes from jumble sales; much cheaper than the local Oxfam which seemed to have gone over to second-hand designer stuff, with prices to match. She had saved a lot of money since persuading her mum that it would be better if she were responsible for buying her own clothes out of an increased allowance. She had put aside something every month; pound after pound, filling up jar after jar. It had taken patience but now was the time; she was ready, ready to leave, ready for the great escape.

Jane kept one foot on her rucksack, out of habit she supposed as there was nobody around to steal it; not that she had anything worth stealing. With none of those trinkets of memory which Jane assumed other people may want around them, her bag held only a few clothes and a wash bag. At the last moment she had put on the red baseball cap, for no other reason than it helped hide her face. By now her eyes must be clashing with the cap, but at least nobody would see.

For a long time Jane stared down into her empty cup; there were no dregs to study, nothing to suggest that her life would get better. The future had to be better, she was certain. But that certainty, like a moment of happiness, vanished as quickly as it had appeared. Things could get a lot worse; somehow that was a comforting thought.

The waitress re-emerged from behind the counter, a cigarette dangling from her mouth and a wet grey rag in her hand. She moved across the room, slip-slopping over the tables as she went. The noise made Jane look up, not fully, just a quick glance from under the cap, but she caught the eye of the waitress.

'You got a problem with the fag? Look, I know I'm not meant to, but there's nobody else around and we have to have our little pleasures, don't we? So if it's OK with you …'

The waitress seemed to want to chat, but Jane did not. Why had she looked up? That was a mistake. As the years had taught her, keep looking down, no eye contact, it was always safer that way.

'You all right love? Somebody upset you have they? Come on, you look as if you wish you'd never been born. It can't be as bad as all that. Want to tell me about it?'

No, thought Jane, *I don't. I don't want to tell you or anybody. I just want to get away, forget everything.*

But that was not so easy for she could still hear Mum's voice. 'You did for me my girl,' that's what her mum had said, over and over again. 'Couldn't have another after you. That was all I wanted, two children, was that too much to ask?'

'I didn't ask to be born. It wasn't my fault that your tubes went wrong.' Though this reply went through Jane's head, it was never spoken.

When her mum was in one of these moods Jane kept quiet; tried to be a comfort, but yet not really be there. She knew, she had always known, that she was a disappointment; that being one was not as good as being two. After a few cigarettes and a little cry, Mum would pull herself together before Dad got home. They both knew that any hint of sadness when he came in would mean trouble. On good days he would grunt, eat his dinner, go to sit in his study and drink quietly. He thought that they did not know about the bottles of whisky he hid in there; they did, but did nothing about it. On bad days he would drink, but not quietly. Any little incident could be the trigger for a row. It was Mum who got the worst of it; Jane keeping very still, trying not to get noticed.

If anybody had asked Jane what she remembered about her childhood, she would have said, had she the strength to answer, that it was shouting, lots of shouting and slamming doors and then silence, a menacing, uneasy, unreal silence. Not that Dad ever hit her mum. Perhaps if he had things would have been different, perhaps then they would have left, Jane and Mum together, to start a new life.

She knew she was inadequate, not what Mum and Dad wanted; everything she said or did seemed to cause an unspoken comparison with an ideal. She was not perfect, but then who was? Still, she tried and tried to please them. Nothing worked; so she became very quiet, almost a shadow.

Sometimes Mum would not blame her for the lack of a sibling but would tell Jane that she was all there was in her life, not that she wanted to live. 'If things get too bad I'll end it you know, got enough pills, just bury me in the garden, it won't matter.' Once Mum described falling out of love with Dad; what a relief it had been, a great weight lifted from her.

'So why are we still here?' Jane had wanted to ask, but could not.

When she was thirteen Jane had discovered the truth. To be more precise she discovered what had happened, for truth requires understanding, not just fact. What she had been looking for and why she searched the bureau, which usually was locked, is now forgotten. What Jane will not forget is finding an old envelope, opening it and staring at her photograph. It was not one she had seen before, but why not, it was no more or less embarrassing than the other baby snaps? Underneath was one of a toddler; good job I'm still not that chubby mused Jane. She looked at the child's eyes; there was something odd about them, something not quite right. Next she found a photograph which she could not understand; there seemed to be two of her, two Janes, in the same shot, a baby and a toddler with Dad holding them both and looking so proud and handsome, and so happy. In a small plastic bag there were locks of hair.

It was then she spotted the newspaper article. 'Tragic death of local children' ran the headline: on the road outside Avignon; collision with a lorry; children did not stand a chance; the baby asleep on her mother's lap in front and the toddler in the back, both straight through the windscreen; died immediately. 'Tiredness was to blame' wrote the reporter and reminded readers to take frequent breaks on long journeys. Jane looked at the date; it was a little under a year before she was born. So Mum had had two children and if they had not died, she, Jane, would not have been born, would not now exist, would not now be the disappointment.

Although everything was put back in its place, Mum must have sensed something when she came back. 'I told him that driving to the South of France in one go was too much, that we should take a break, but he would have it his own way, as usual.' Mum looked into the distance. 'They took away my babies, my beautiful babies. I only wanted to hold them but they took them away.'

Jane had crept out and in her room vowed to leave; she had to escape, but how? If she ran away where would she go? Anyway, at thirteen the police would bring her back wouldn't they? So Jane waited and saved, saved and waited, and now, three years later, she had some money and a handful of GCSEs. That is why she was here, in this shabby buffet waiting for the train to London which would take her to a new life, to build new memories.

Like pre-waking dreams, Jane's reflections had taken but an instant. 'Come on love, cheer up. Do you want another cup of tea?' asked the waitress, who by now was getting rather concerned and wonders if she should do something, but as she cannot think what, puts the idea aside. 'Had a row with your boyfriend have you? Going back to your ma so she can make it better?'

'No, I ... well, it's not like that.' Jane wished that she did not have to speak, but felt it would be impolite not to. The waitress seemed not to have heard; seeing misery on the face of another had sparked a mood of self pity.

'You're lucky to have a mother, try being brought up in an orphanage, then you'd have nowhere to go back to, nowhere to call home.'

'I think my train's about due, I'd better get organised.' Grateful for this reason to leave, Jane gathered up her rucksack and walked out with determination in her step. The neon of the buffet cast an eerie light over the platform. Inside the waitress carried on cleaning the tables; the dirty cloth wiping away her thoughts with the spilt sugar. In the distance a couple clasped one another, holding onto their last moments together. Somewhere out in the night a dog barked; the rest was silent. The train pulled in, the yellow glow of the carriages promising a safe, warm haven.

Jane waited for the doors to open, then, throwing the rucksack over her shoulder, she turned and walked back toward the ticket office. *After all,* she thought, *Mum needs me, doesn't she?*

Tales From A Pariah's Path

Sebastian Tristan Henry Lumly-Graybow Tudor

Ezekiel Zeev sat in his old Charger making his way, at speed, towards his apartment. Next to him sat Leander, a shotgun aimed at the squirming body bag on the back seat. The engine roared as he sped down the final stretch. He spun the car into the parking space outside his apartment and got out Leander, covering the body bag all the while. They dragged it out and got it up the stairs to Ezekiel's apartment. Leander threw the door open and took aim again with his shotgun as Ezekiel dragged the body bag into the room. He dropped it into the middle of the room and drew a berretta from inside his long jacket and took aim at the squirming body bag.

The bag ripped open and a thin, lanky creature pulled itself to its feet, it looked at the two of them and hissed. Leander squeezed the trigger of his shotgun and sent a shell into the creature's stomach sending it flying into the wall behind it. He grinned toothily. 'Hey Zeke, I got 'im an' I'm pretty sure he ain't gettin' up any time soon.' He looked back at the creature to find that despite having a large amount of its abdomen next to it on the floor, it was still determinedly getting to its feet, anger written all over its hideous face. Leander pumped his shotgun and fired another round into the creature then repeated the action.

Ezekiel had moved towards the creature, after Leander had stopped, to see if it was dead. He kicked it and it sprang at Leander. Leander took aim and pulled the trigger of his shotgun but found that he was out of ammo; instead he smashed the creature across its face with the butt of it. This didn't stop the creature from throwing Leander to the floor and attempting to sink its teeth into his throat.

Leander bared his teeth and growled. Hair started growing all over his body, he seemed to become more muscular and his eyes and teeth became distinctly feline. He threw the relatively small creature into the air and sprang from the floor showing that a furry tail had burst through the seat of his trousers. He looked, his hands and claws shot from the ends of his fingers. The creature seemed completely unperturbed by this and shot towards him again. Leander drove his claws into the creature's sides as it pushed him to the floor again. It tried going for his throat again. There was the sound of metal on flesh and then the smell of cold steel and fresh blood floated on the air. The creature's head rolled off its shoulders. Behind it Leander could see Ezekiel with a long sword in hand, a trickle of blood on the blade.

'Next time Lee, just remember that its head will come off fairly easily. OK?'

Leander nodded and got to his feet slowly shaking off the effects of his transformation. 'Why didn't ya do that earlier, Zeke?'

'Because it was necessary for those people standing around to think that this guy was really dead and that we were there to help him. We need to wait for the ...'

The phone in the corner of the room rang. Zeke picked it up and listened to what the person on the other end had to say then dropped the receiver. 'Come on, we've got to get out of here, one of the neighbours called the police because they heard gunfire.'

His accusatory tone made Leander lower his head in embarrassment. Ezekiel opened the window and jumped out onto the fire escape. Leander followed, dropping a grenade belt behind him. He smiled as the two of them got in Ezekiel's car and the upper floors of the apartment block exploded, bricks, glass and the floors above raining down on the bystanders below.

Ezekiel sped away.

On the way Ezekiel's phone rang. He reached onto the small area of back seat and pulled the phone free of his jacket. He flipped it open and put it to his ear. 'This is Zeev.'

'A pariah is required at the Echo Organics Food Group building.'

'What do we know?'

'So far we know that there are two people dead and it looks more like an animal attack. A pariah of the third order will meet you there.'

'That won't be necessary Proteus.'

'Really? Well I think someone who still follows the rules should be around to ensure you don't cause anymore problems. I mean, did you really need to take out the entire building when removing a V-type?'

'Leander thought it was necessary. And at least there won't be any evidence.'

'I agree, a lack of evidence is a good thing but we didn't want any humans injured and there are several people still trapped underneath the rubble. I don't care what you say Zeev, you will be met by a third order and you will do your job!' The phone went dead. Zeev flipped the cover down and threw it over his shoulder onto his jacket. He sighed and looked at Leander. 'We've got a new friend for this next one.'

'Not another sixth order. We had one of those children before, can't someone else teach those babies?'

'Don't worry, we've got a third order.'

'That won't be as bad as long as they go along with what we tell them to do.'

'Hmm ... unfortunately this time they will be making sure we follow the rules.'

'You're f****** jokin'! Please tell me you're jokin'!' Zeev smiled and went back to watch the road.

Outside the towering building of the Echo Organics Food Group, hundreds of police officers barred the entrance from the journalists and other onlookers. Zeev pulled up down the street. Leander and he came round and sat on the bonnet of the Charger. A woman dressed in a very loose shirt and an almost indecent denim skirt walked up to them. Leander looked her over. 'Sorry, not tonight love.'

'How dare you? I am of the third order of the pariah.'

Leander's jaw dropped. Zeev couldn't help but smirk.

'The High Caste in New York thought you needed to be watched and reminded that humans aren't the enemy and that the rules are there for a reason.'

'Okay, but what's with the f*****' get up?' Leander looked her up and down again.

She frowned. 'The officer in charge of the investigation is somewhat crooked and is fairly fond of the company of women from street corners. I will distract him whilst you two find out what you can from inside. Remember no humans are to be killed.' Leander grinned as she turned and left.

'Did she say anythin' about damagin' humans, Zeke?'

'No.' Leander's face lit up at the response.

Two police officers flew through the fire door, closely followed by Leander in his altered state. He sprang to his feet and delivered a savage kick to the side of one of the officer's heads and slammed his elbow into the other's throat. Two more officers came running down the hallway. Zeev came through the fire door, pistol raised. He shot both of them at speed, hardly looking at them.

'That was cold,' grunted Leander.

Zeev holstered the gun and kept walking down the corridor. There was one officer left outside the crime scene. His gun was already raised and pointed at Zeev. Zeev kept walking. The officer gave no warning, he just pulled the trigger. Three bullets hit Zeev. He kept walking. The officer emptied the remainder of the clip into him. Zeev kept walking. The officer reached for another magazine but Zeev pushed his hand into the officer's nose slamming the back of his head into the wall, blood spraying the floor from the officer's nose. Zeev kicked open the door and entered. Leander followed but stopped to look at the police officer. He shook his head and followed him.

Zeev drew his sword from under his long jacket. Leander sniffed the air and shrugged. 'Too much human blood in the air to smell anything else Zeke?'

'Yeah?'

'What the hell was that back there? I've never seen you get shot up before. You just walked it off. That can't be healthy?'

'His bullets couldn't do any damage to me so I thought I'd take him out in a quieter fashion.' Leander grunted and walked down one of the two hallways that led away from the entrance. Zeev raised his sword and took the other. His eyes took a few seconds to grow accustomed to the gloom, but afterwards he managed to make out bloody hand and claw prints all over the walls of the passageway. He looked at the floor to see droplets of blood all over the carpet. He came into the living room. The floorboards creaked behind him. He spun on his heel, sword at the ready. Leander had frozen behind him, his hands up. Zeev relaxed. Leander moved further into the room and waved for Zeev to come over to him.

Zeev walked over to him and looked over Leander's huge shoulder. 'Zeke, what do you make of this?' He pointed at long trails of strange smelling saliva on the carpet that was on the whole devoid of bloodstains.

'Could be the proof we need to connect this to the para' activity in the area. Here, get a sample,'

Zeev passed Leander a small sample bottle from within his jacket with which he scooped up a small amount of the saliva. He handed it back to Zeev who put the sample back into his jacket. Zeev made his way into the kitchen area. There lay the body of Maximillian Echo, the owner of the Echo Organics Food Group. There was less than half of the man's body left and that was spread over the whole kitchen unit. Over the floor lay half of his intestines, some of his brain was sprayed onto the oven door. Three of his fingers were clutching a cupboard handle. One eye lay next to what may have been the remains of his foot. Bite marks ran the length of his spinal cord that had been completely picked clean of meat, tooth marks showing clearly on the bone.

Zeev turned away, an unimpressed expression on his face. He walked into the bathroom. Inside he found the shredded body of Echo's girlfriend. Her body was still mostly intact but her back had very deep claw marks in it, and her stomach had been torn open down to her crotch. Above her head was a long sacrificial dagger that had been driven into the wall. Leander shot into the room and cringed. 'Ouch! Zeev a load more cops are on their way in here, we gotta go.'

Zeev turned and walked out into the living room again. He faced the window. He rushed at it and made a swing with his sword. It seemed not to touch it but after a second or two the window fell from its frame. Zeev dived out, Leander followed, several bullets whizzing past his head.

They both hit the ground hard. Zeev was on his feet in seconds and was hauling Leander's immense bulk back to his car. Hana Gytha came sprinting after them and dived through the door into the back seat as Zeev threw Leander in the passenger seat. Zeev got into the driver's seat and started the car. When he looked up he saw a cop with a tyre shredder. He put his foot down as hard as possible. The car lurched into action.

The cop threw the shredder. Zeev's tyres hit the spikes. The car flipped, rolled and exploded. Flames flew into the air, the shockwave from the blast knocking back the closest officers. Zeev sat in the flaming car and closed his eyes as his lungs began to fill with smoke.

The Reunion

Mary McGuigan

Howard Carter, a handsome, prosperous-looking businessman in his late fifties, relaxed in a corner seat as the last train carried him swiftly away from the city. It had been a stressful day but, finally, a deal had been completed that would add more wealth to his already comfortable income. Diamonds were his business, mostly above-board and strictly regulated but, on the other side, he bought and sold illicit stones and engaged in the excitingly dangerous trade of financing sales of arms to the Far East. His business associates were not aware of this; frequent journeyings abroad were part of the scene; they all had to undertake such trips. His busy day had ended with a customary visit to his favourite girlfriend, a nice dinner in her flat, followed by a satisfactory session in the bedroom. On the train later, he reflected on how he had manipulated his lifestyle, from a convict working in the mines to where he was now, comfortably situated, in a middle-class environment. But on the train, too, was a watcher intent on following him - to the ends of the earth if need be.

Howard walked home through the leafy suburbs of his small town and entered his pleasant driveway. The watcher had no difficulty in sheltering among the trees and shrubs. *All in good order,* thought the proud owner. *Must remember to tell Alice she was right about the new gardener.*

Opening the door, he made for his study. His wife, he knew, would be fast asleep upstairs, and would not wish to be disturbed. With a pleasant feeling of relief at being home again, he closed the door and went to a safe in the wall. It was concealed behind a painting of one of his wife's ancestors. He inserted his code card. The safe revealed things that he considered were his escape route, if that became necessary. A large bundle of bank notes, false papers and passport, a small, lethal-looking revolver and, at the back, a small leather-bound box.

He brought out the box and spread the contents onto his desk: there were a quantity of uncut diamonds. The next thing was a drink, a glass of excellent brandy. He drank one, and poured out a second draught of the amber liquid. He caressed and examined the diamonds. With his expert knowledge, he knew his finances were sound for the rest of his life. He sipped the brandy, and then was aware of a feeling of apprehension in the room; an atmosphere he'd not noticed before.

Getting up, he went round the study and, drawing the curtains, was amazed to find the French door open. This had never happened before; Alice was meticulous in the extreme. Putting it down to a rare oversight, he locked the door and returned to his diamonds. Still the feeling persisted that he was not alone, then, finishing off the second drink, he was aware of a sort of noise outside the door. Now thoroughly alarmed, he threw the precious gems in their box and quickly put them back in the safe, but his arms felt strangely wooden, and he was unable to close it. Then he saw the door of the study slowly opening. Howard wanted to call his wife, but seemed to be struck dumb. Alice, however, was not asleep in her room; she was not even in the house. He had quite forgotten she had gone to stay with her aged aunt for a couple of days.

Lately, she had been reflecting on her life since marriage. Her appearance was pleasant, a trim woman of middle height, with dark hair and expressive, grey eyes, she presented a calm and rather dignified personality. The daughter of a retired clergyman, her life had been somewhat sheltered. She had worked locally for a friend of her father, and became his secretary. Earlier, she had had a number of boyfriends, but they all seemed to her to be quite juvenile. Life went pleasantly on for Alice until her father became frail. She decided to give up her job and look after him. This situation worked very well; they had much in common.

One day, visiting various houses, she called on Howard Carter, having heard he was newly in the district and apparently well-off. He instantly liked the look of the woman who was collecting money for repairs to the church, her lady-like and pleasant demeanour impressed him. When Alice's father died, Howard made it his business to assist her in various ways. She was glad of the moral support he offered, and felt less lonely, as she had been a devoted daughter. Some time later, Howard proposed marriage, and was accepted. For him, it was mostly a matter of convenience and status; for her, an exciting prospect.

When they had settled down in the new house, the marriage, for Alice, eventually became a great disappointment. Howard was utterly self-centred, and quite unaware of the soft and affectionate side to her nature. He worked in the city every day, sometimes abroad, Alice was again a rather lonely person; but she continued to run the house and garden quietly and efficiently.

After a few years, a child was born, but the baby lived for only a few months. Howard was secretly thankful, but Alice retired further into her shell.

One day, she was busy in the garden, her main delight, when a voice said, 'You look as though you could do with a hand.' She had been struggling with a rampant shrub in the drive, and was finding it a tough proposition. The voice belonged to a lean man of medium height, his face rather weather-beaten, with a scar on one side. He was quietly spoken and had the most arrestingly blue eyes that Alice had ever seen. When he moved, she noticed he walked with a slight limp.

On hearing he was looking for garden work, she took him on without hesitation. They were both interested in growing things. Robert Gates knew a lot about the subject, and Alice was relieved to have someone to do the hard work that gardening entails.

The months went by. They developed a friendship; he was a sensitive man, quite unlike her husband. She found herself looking forward to his twice-weekly visits. When the weather was poor, they sat in the kitchen, drinking tea, and Robert told her about his life and near-death experience in Africa. Slowly, an intimacy developed between them. He had not sought to hide the disreputable part of his life, whereas she knew nothing of Howard's past, except that most of his time had been spent abroad. Alice realised that the empathy between herself and Robert was deepening into something more than she had ever dreamed could happen. This quietly-spoken man possessed many of the qualities of her father - resolution, sincerity, as well as a dry, sometimes impish sense of humour; his rare smile touched her heart.

'That's my story, Harry. What a way to treat your old partner! Remember, once, I'd saved your life. After the explosion and fire in the mine, you left me with dreadful injuries. You left me for dead, but you didn't even bother to find out, or whether I burnt alive, or not. You escaped, somehow, with my share of the diamonds we'd stashed away. I've waited twenty years for this, and I'm going to enjoy every minute.' Howard, by now, was petrified, his whole world collapsing in front of the man who should have died all those years ago.

'How … how … ?' he stuttered, but the words wouldn't come. The other man continued in a cold, matter-of-fact voice. 'They thought I was a goner. I spent two years in the prison hospital. They reckoned I'd served my time and threw me out. Helpless, like a baby, I was. The orderly who'd looked after me took pity. We went back to his father, who was the witch doctor in his village.' At this, Howard, filled with dread, unable to move a muscle, was deathly pale and couldn't speak. The man continued, 'I was there over two years, Harry, they saved my life. You wouldn't believe the things they can do, and the things they use to cure people, and a lot of it works. Before you go, and you *are* going, the poison in your drink is tasteless and can't be traced. It's from a plant that only grows in one place in Africa.' Howard could only just hear his former partner. His strength quite gone, his life rapidly ebbing, he heard, 'At last I'm getting back what you owe me. Alice knows all this; I'm the gardener. We're very good friends. She won't be a grieving widow for long.'

A Question Of Perspective: The Camera And The Hat

Peter G T Schapira

They came to stare.

They crowded in the cold white gallery, inching their way forwards. Snaking round the exhibits, a hushed burble echoed the hallowed halls. A new exhibition using Jakob's third eye was always an event in this small provincial town which had only ever produced one son of note - and he had vanished.

The large photographs sprawled across the walls drawing the viewers into monochrome vistas they had never imagined: vast expanses of undulating desert, pock marked with nomadic feet; claustrophobic encasements of sky high trees through which pale shafts of light glinted, an animal feeding ground, a human killing ground; round wide-eyed faced of children in front of mud hutted homes stared back.

A boy, bored with the black and white, struggled free from the grasping parental hand and went in search of colour.

Nobody had noticed the mahogany bench in the centre of the gallery on which a camera and a hat were carefully placed. He went up to it, fingers itching, but dared not touch. He tiptoed round it. The camera was old, its long revealing, some time intrusive, eye asleep. The straw hat, weather beaten and grubby, looked out of place. It could be a hippo in a mud bath, a camel hump, or a sand hill rising out of the earthy ground, chuckled the boy as he stood at one end of the bench, and then the other.

'There you are!' exclaimed the harassed mother. 'What have you found now?'

'Look at this, an old camera and a hat on a bench,' said the boy cheerfully, innocently ignoring the trouble he might have caused.

As soon as he spoke, heads turned. Strangers wandered over and solemnly stood around the bench, heads to one side and then the other. Half closed eyes measured up the significant of the positioning.

'Fascinating ...'

'Such resonance ...'

'To have such a life-like sculpture adds such relevance ...'

'It sits there viewing the viewers - quite unnerving really ...'

The comments rose to a pitch and then fell away as people moved on. The boy shook his head, he really didn't understand quite what all the fuss was about as he was led out by the possessive hand.

No one saw the hunched old man pick up the camera, carefully hang it around his neck and place the moth-eaten hat on his head and leave by the entrance which they had all passed through.

The boy turned to have one last look at his camel humped hippo on a sand hill. All he saw was a piece of card which read: 'The camera is my eyes and my memory and you have remembered me by coming here. Like God, what was here, showed the world to you as it is, what you have made it, what you are and what you will be again. The camera lets you forget until you open up its memory'.

Great Potential

(In memory of Doctor Laffin PHD)

Gerard Allardyce

Perhaps Andrew's most telling memory of academic work came in the first year of sixth form. He had completed twelve hours of 3 mock 'A' level papers. The fact he had sat them at all was a miracle because he had only passed his geography 'O' level at Christmas, on the third attempt.

It was after the general sociology master had given out the results on which he had featured last, with a 'D' grade, that a few words of encouragement were perhaps in order.

It was in the Caton Gallery that this much-decorated officer (and holder of the Military Cross) had a few words with Andrew. Andrew held this military historian in great respect.

'Do you know Andrew, you wrote more than anyone else in the general sociology papers, but unfortunately you gave a literary critique instead of a balanced argument and analysis of the sociologist content.' Andrew didn't take much notice of this constructive criticism. In his mind he was still riding high on the success of his geography paper last Christmas. His 'A' level teacher both in general sociology and English literature considered he had 'great potential'. At this point, Andrew switched off. He believed wholeheartedly that he had 'great potential', what need for work? He would muddle through. And then, as he wandered through the school's gardens that were modelled on le Notre in Versailles, he reflected on a ghost from the past.

There had been a Mr Pearson. He came from an agency to be a teacher at the school and held double masters from Perth University in Australia and All Souls in Oxford. Everyone had looked forward to Michael Pearson's appointment in classics and history. Then slowly and irrevocably he went mad. Then came the day when Mr Pearson locked himself in the loos. The crisis was excellently managed by the senior boys who escorted the sick man to the headmaster, who in turn helped him to the waiting ambulance. That night at supper the headmaster described Mr Pearson as a 'loveable man, loved by everyone in the school'. He was now in the excellent care of the hospital. It was all over but the man who was the teacher, much-decorated soldier and military historian said to Andrew. 'You will end up like him if you are not very careful.'

It was a comment that left Andrew cold. What could he do? There was another year of 'A' levels to go, wouldn't it be nice to go on holiday, to run away? Then he remembered his six year stay at an independent grammar school deep in the heart of the Sussex Weald. He remembered his first term, homesick and wandering in a daze in the dusk of the evening in the leafy grounds of the school. He remembered one particular winter's night, a dense fog encompassing the lights of the gym where a group of the sixth form were listening to a record on the stage and drinking lager. The song? 'Ferry Across The Mersey' by Gerry and the Pacemakers. But it was not just the song of course, but the whole advent of the Beetles in 1964 when he was finding that should have changed his life. 1964-1970, he went to the boarding school at the inception of the Labour Government and in 1970 left the school as they left office, in a daze. How his father had praised Harold Wilson, the Premier in 1964. 'He has appointed an Ambassador to China, Andrew,' his father had said with true admiration. 'Everyone had been well off in the sixties,' his father had told Andrew, 'everyone had money in their pockets, but what now?'

Andrew's father figure was no longer Prime Minister and he was about to go to college in Liverpool after a single scratch pass in history had secured him a place at teacher training college. The headmaster had chosen this place for him because like his two schools it was a sheltered environment run by priests and nuns.

'Do you really want to go to this college in Liverpool?' his father asked in all seriousness. Then as a rejoinder, 'Don't you think it would be better if you secured a little job for yourself in the Inland Revenue as a clerical assistant and then worked your way up?'

'No, I want to go to college,' came Andrew's weary reply.

'Very well,' his father said with an air of resignation, 'then you must go to college.'

Within seven months, from September to March, Andrew had literally gone through college like a dose of salts and found himself caught in a complete whirlwind.

The Quest from the outset, was a date, but then when that didn't materialise and the academic work became harder, the two fused and his brain snapped. Perhaps it was too much to bear having beautiful girls around him and having to start and complete assignments that were just too difficult. Two months prior to leaving the college he found himself a recluse, reading through referrals by a senior student. Dostoevsky's novel 'Crime and Punishment', he read it from page to page, cover to cover. When he finished the book, he had a beard of four days growth and he celebrated his pyrrhic achievement by drinking a bottle of vodka and smoking a packet of Sobranie Black Russian cigarettes.

'It's a shame. You can't tell him,' said one student to another.

In March there followed, for Andrew, a primary admission to the psychiatric wing of the Sefton General Hospital. The Sister was handing out the medicine from the trolley. She looked immaculate in her blue uniform. She gave Andrew a Sodium Anatole to help him sleep. In effect it was a powerful sleeping drug. As he began to lose consciousness Andrew remembered the words of his special teacher, 'You have great potential', and then he remembered, 'You will end up like him if you are not very careful'.

And so he had. But for Andrew the fight for survival had begun. There was a question, where would he affix his flag for the stand of life?

The Mental Breakdown

C Le Breton

Victoria slammed the boot of her car shut and lowered the heavy shopping bags to the floor. She straightened up again to push her hair out of her face and wondered what on earth had possessed her to go food shopping, on what forecasters were calling the hottest day of the year so far.

With a sigh she picked up the heavy bags and walked up the driveway to her front door. As she approached, she noticed the door to be ajar. With alarm Victoria dropped the shopping bags where she was and ran inside. The downstairs of the house appeared just as she'd left it. With fear rising in her stomach she headed for the stairs. She checked the bedrooms and then moved towards the bathroom door. As she opened it, a gasp caught in her throat. She leant on the sink to steady herself, for there before her very eyes in the bathtub lay her husband, dead. Appearing to have drowned.

Now she knew what had possessed her to go shopping.

Trying to steady herself, her eyes searched diligently for the knife wounds on him. She remembered fetching the stiletto knife, the slim one with the sharp point on the end of it, also the row before leaving the house, one of many that they had regularly.

He had been particularly annoying that morning. Demanding, and treating her as one of his servants. His mind had been quickening up for months, an exact replica of once before, when his first breakdown occurred.

Victoria had lived through several of these sessions; the doctor said it was stress, thus giving him tablets. What had they done for her? Nothing, as usual. Always presuming that she could cope. The strong wife supporting her sick husband, she didn't need any help.

Unfortunately she had snapped this time; he had gone too far and in a rage she had stabbed him with the stiletto knife from the kitchen. The problem was she could see no blood, surely there should be some blood in the bath water?

Moving hesitantly towards the body, Victoria looked closer in the bath. No! She could see neither knife wounds nor blood, how strange. What had she done with the knife? Looking around the bathroom carefully there was no sign of it.

How strange: did she dream it all, or was she going mad? Living with him was enough to send a saint mad, he never gave his nagging or criticisms a rest. He just went on and on, winding her up until she could scream.

This behaviour sometimes gave her loss of memory, also the fact of only being able to hear from one ear properly. It had helped her survive the past tormenting years from him.

She found herself smiling as she stood looking down at the dead body. 'Well, Victoria,' she said to herself, 'you won't have him mentally abusing you again.' But she was still puzzled. No knife wounds, the front door ajar, and the lack of blood which should have been present.

All Victoria could remember was going out of the front door and getting into the car. Nothing much about what might have happened earlier. Did she close the front door properly? She was sure, or nearly sure, he had been in the bedroom. Rushing as quickly as her legs would allow she checked the unmade bed, floor, and dressing table for the knife and any signs of blood. Standing still, she tried to get her brain into gear. It seemed to have stopped altogether.

What was she going to do? How could she explain to the police what had happened, because Victoria was not altogether sure herself. With her mind a blank, she took one more look at her husband's dead body in the bath, then went downstairs to make herself a cup of tea. Seeing the front door open, with the dropped shopping bags by the door, she proceeded to pick them up and shut the front door behind her.

Going into the kitchen she put her shopping on the table, filling the kettle and switching it on. The knife; where was it? These thoughts entered her head, so leaving the shopping where it was she went to search for the knife.

Looking to where they were kept in the rack, she diligently went through them all. Examining each one, she found there were none missing, nor any bloodstained ones.

Whatever had happened that morning, perhaps it was the heat. Stopping the search to put her shopping away, she realised how lucky she was not to have any frozen food in it. With the sweat pouring off her, she made the tea and looking up at the clock, saw she had been home an hour. Surely the normal reaction would have been to call the police straight away. How would she explain that to them?

With her mind in a complete muddle now, the sweat was really pouring off her. Sitting at the kitchen table, she began to sip her tea.

Victoria could remember how angry she had felt whilst leaving the house, also how she had wished him dead when driving away into town.

Arriving in town, she couldn't remember the journey, only arriving and parking the car. Then the memories of that dreadful row, the cruel words uttered in anger.

Perhaps he didn't mean it? Perhaps her wish had come true? This meant she had a life without him forever now. If this was murder by her own hand, how it would be on her conscience for life.

Perhaps she would get a prison sentence, or maybe let off for diminished responsibility. There were no feelings at all for the dead body in the bath.

He hadn't been a bad man, she thought, *so why were there no feelings left?* This was her husband she had found, there were questions to be answered, which she couldn't do. Only her muddled mind took over.

Having finished her cup of tea, she automatically went to the phone, picked it up and called the police. Then standing up, she wandered around the lounge, not actually knowing what was going on around her.

Was it shock? she thought. *Or guilt, but how could it be guilt?* She was out at the time. These thoughts just swam around her head, there was no blood, no wound, so how could she have killed him? The world had turned upside down, but she felt at peace, no remorse, or guilt.

She was in a state of limbo. As she waited for the police to arrive, suddenly all the stresses of the past years melted away forever. The torment that she took in silence, telling nobody, as he was known by the outside world as such a pleasant fellow. But why should she tell anybody? It was betraying her marriage and her husband. A great weight had been lifted off her shoulders, and she could now begin her life, whatever was in front of her. Victoria was now unafraid of the future.

Last Day For The Goose Girl

Paul May

When my mother called, I answered her immediately. I shouted back and that morning I answered all her questions. I answered my father's questions and the questions of my grandmother. I listened keenly to what they said and then I answered and all the time, I thought about him. I tried to think about him in the air of late winter and early spring that breathed around me.

When morning began to whistle, I rose and I stepped out into a morning that breathed the changing of the seasons. He had said that he would meet me at the train station in the city and the whistle of the train was the whistle that I felt I could hear in the country air and that air spoke of new hope and new dreams, and the dreams that smelt of the past were beginning to be filled with a new hope.

When he first came to the country, he reminded me of a relative who grew up in the country, who went away and then returned and as I knew him, he was the same. He had the blood of the country. He spoke of escape, longing and the air that breathed through the country and which breathed into the city, but I was going away. That was what mattered and it was right. It was morning. There was sadness and longing, but there was no hope. When I looked at my mother and then at my father, that was what I saw, sadness, longing, but hope as well, and I knew I was right and I knew that amidst the sadness there was happiness. I felt that, I think for months, and now it was clear. The air was tinged with sadness. All that I would leave behind.

* * * * * *

You are leaving behind a lot, I thought. *Goose Girl leaves it all behind.* That was it and when I thought about the country paths, I thought now that we never walked through them. We never walked along the paths that surrounded her house and that surrounded my house. Because they were not paths that we were meant to take. I remember one night with her. The sun was dying. I knew I felt the redness in the sky. As I look back, the red blood of the sky was in the distance and that meant that there was no sky above. In an atmosphere that was not quiet or serene, there was no hope.

I came back.

The goose girl had hope in her eyes. Goose girl. You couldn't see her in the evening and she was hidden but she wasn't trying to hide and she stepped out and walked quietly over and I walked to her. She is a goose girl. She chose to follow the dream in her and the longing and the hope that burn in her.

One day, she said to put everything behind in the past. This was the past. We were now chasing dreams into the future. Dreams that were fragile and ethereal. There wasn't room or space for much. There was room for hope but no room for the past.

'We'll go together,' she said.

'We'll go together,' I said quietly.

'OK, we'll go, this is right,' she said.

Right. But she didn't know what it meant and that was what I liked about her. She didn't understand right and wrong. Other girls did and they decided to choose wrong. She didn't know but she was always right and when I was with her, I walked with her the right path. That was why I began to think of her as the goose girl. She followed the right path. She was alone. With her mother, her father and family, she was alone.

I said, 'You're independent.'

'Am I?' she smiled.

She had gone away to the city to work. That was where I met her. I thought of other girls.

'You're not independent.'

She had hope in her eyes like a goose girl. She had a younger brother who she brought with her on some walks. I knew that. I never walked with her. Maybe I knew the paths that she walked. I was also waiting for her. I knew that she wanted to escape her home. I couldn't understand properly her longing. Maybe it was the longing of a goose girl, a shepherdess who looks out into the evening air and feels the light in the air or feels the moonlight and I couldn't understand that and I didn't want to understand it.

* * * * * *

I was sitting with friends and I told them that he was waiting. 'Waiting,' I said, 'waiting.' But he wasn't really waiting.

'Is he waiting?' one asked.

'No, he's not waiting,' I answered. Then we were quiet.

'When are you going?'

She knew that day I was going. She meant what time.

'I'm going in the morning,' and I thought then I was going in the morning when they would all be asleep.

'We'll miss you.'

'I'll miss you all, come on,' and we hugged.

My mother said later, 'You are very beautiful,' and a boy I knew said that he would miss me. That was when I knew it was right. I looked into this young man's eyes. He was just a friend but when he said that he would miss me, I felt I knew what he meant and I felt that I would miss him. I looked into my mother's eyes and thought I would miss her, but I would be coming back.

One night later, I met the young man again and I thought if anything happened to him, I would miss him and I thought deeper and deeper, *I will miss him,* and then I thought about the others, not my family, and I thought, *I won't miss them.*

* * * * * *

'Will we meet after Christmas?' she asked. It was then I thought how her longing was different to others. She was different to others. When I tried to escape from the past, I went into her life. I knew then what longing was, which I never knew. I thought that I knew what longing and love were, but I know now that I just thought I knew. I was wrong and the wrong filled my life for a long time. I didn't understand. I worked hard and I filled my life with work.

'I saw her coming into my life, the Goose Girl,
I saw her coming into my life, the Goose Girl,
I saw her on her path,
I saw her away from me leading her brother down the path,
Goose Girl call, Goose Girl call.'

* * * *

That evening, she sat with her family for a while and then she went to her room. She prepared to go. She waited quietly into the night.

Away in the evening air, he thought about the future.

'This is right'.

Past - Revisited

T G Bloodworth

The two brothers breasted the slopes of Mallow Hill, a local beauty spot. Once or twice a year they made the pilgrimage to where their parents' ashes had been scattered. Looking down at the small valley, they could see Stepping Stones, a large house. Some sixty-odd years ago this had been their home, and held many happy memories.

Once again they rested and reminisced. Thomas and George Martin, though brothers, were totally different. As lads, Thomas, the elder, was quiet and impressionable. George on the other hand was quite the opposite, running everywhere, very vocal and invariably made a nuisance of himself. As usual they talked about the past, each prompting the other when memory failed.

Not far from Stepping Stones lay Milton Farm. George recalled Farmer Merrydew.

'Miserable old sod,' said Thomas, 'because of him our dog was put down, alleged sheep worrying. Anyway, he got all he deserved.'

'Funny,' said George, 'he always claimed he was innocent. What was the name of the chap he shot?'

'Charlie Townsend,' said Thomas. 'He was found in the road, shot through the head, his bicycle in the ditch, they never found the gun, but the jury found Merrydew guilty, and consequently he was hanged. Apparently he had a pistol registered to him, as a member of the Home Guard. When asked to produce it, the gun had gone missing.'

George laughed. 'Strange thing is I remember the day it happened. Gramp went ballistic, his daily newspaper went missing. It was April 1st, he blamed me thinking I tried to April fool him.'

Stepping Stones was owned then by their paternal grandfather. William, the lads' father, had run his business from home, a small milk round. Using one of the old outhouses as a dairy, where he sterilised all his equipment, no bottles in those days.

Thomas smiled, 'Gramp never found his paper, but Father wasn't happy either. His leather bag for collecting the milk money also disappeared from the dairy, fortunately there was no money in it.'

Gazing around, Thomas and George both commented on various changes to the landscape, how it was and how it used to be when they were young. As they began their descent, Jackson's Quarry could be seen about 1.5 miles away.

'Remember the owl?' said Thomas.

George grinned, 'As if I could forget!'

About a year before the 'Townsend incident', Thomas, George and another lad, Frank Miles, had visited the quarry, looking for birds' eggs. In those days it was an acceptable hobby. Thomas and Frank helped George, being smallest, up to a large hole, almost cave-like, to see if any nests were present. A large owl flew out in his face, no damage was done, but the occasion never forgotten.

Moving on down the hill, Thomas said, 'Mother always thought Charlie Townsend was a German spy. I overheard her talking to Dad once, but Father said it was most unlikely.'

'One less then,' said George, 'if it was true.'

Glancing back up Mallow Hill, they both nodded. All being well they would return next year, but each year, the slopes seemed steeper.

It was some five years later that Thomas passed away. With his papers and documents, including a will, was a sealed letter addressed to George. 'Probably some last request,' said George to his son, Andrew. 'Your Uncle Thomas could always be counted on for the unexpected.'

The letter was straightforward, George was requested to visit Jackson Quarry, just once more to see if the owl was still at home, it was possible he might find something to his advantage.

George shook his head. 'If he thinks I'm climbing that quarry again, he's got another thought coming.'

'You have to go,' said Andrew, 'it's a last request. If you like I'll climb the quarry, just show me where it is.'

So George and Andrew set off, passing Mallow Hill on the way. Arriving at the quarry, George pointed to a large hole half way up the face. Andrew took off his coat, rolled his sleeves up and started to climb. All went well, as Andrew approached the hole, George shouted out, 'Mind the owl.' Andrew gave a wave in acknowledgement.

He peered into the hole, then reached in, his head out of sight. On re-emerging, he had something in his hand. George, waiting at the bottom, urged Andrew to take his time. Safely at the bottom, George and Andrew examined their find.

'Good heavens, it looks like Father's old leather milk round bag and still in good condition,' cried George.

Slowly George undid the leather strap. Inside it appeared to be an old newspaper wrapped around something. Date on the newspaper was April 1st 1942. George gasped; inside the paper was an old pistol!

The Power Of Love

Audrey Allen

I started to walk quickly, night was falling fast; there was a strange atmosphere in the air tonight, I can't explain what or why, but it was there. I laughed to myself, it was so unlike me to give way to feelings; as a vicar's wife, I had grown quite tough. I can remember as if it were yesterday, arriving here with my handsome husband John, his dark eyes sparkling, he was so excited, so happy, this was his first parish as a young vicar and my first home as a new bride; we had been married just a month. Yes! Over the last ten years I had become confident and able to face most things; but tonight ... I don't know.

I had walked this way so many times, after visiting my good friend Jane, a shortcut from her house to the vicarage, a large rambling old house yet dwarfed by the 200-year-old church standing floodlit in the vast churchyard, with its old gravestones casting giant shadows on the church walls - like people about to move or to speak.

Then my footsteps began to slow down; in the distance at the end of the path, the only way to the vicarage, was the dark figure of a man. From a distance I could not see his face but I knew he was stood by a newly-dug grave. I had seen the gardener digging it earlier this morning; he had spoken to me asking me to wish the vicar good luck as he travelled to London to ask for money for the new boiler. We had managed to raise about three-quarters of the cost, but we needed the rest so that we could complete the arrangements with a local contractor as soon as possible as they were anxious to commence work in the very near future; their quotation had been the lowest and we were desperate for the new boiler.

As I was talking to the gardener, I remember thinking how deep the hole he was digging was, perhaps it was for two people. With the sun shining on it, it looked ... well, just a hole, but now as I thought about it I shivered. It seemed sinister as I stood here in the dusk of the evening wondering who the figure was, standing motionless by the newly-dug grave. Then my mind went into overdrive; who was the grave for? John had not told me of any burials from our parish, but there was no reason why he should; our churchyard was still used for quite a wide area. John dealt with all and anything concerning the church, quite often with the local council on behalf of people who once lived in this parish. So ... well, my dilemma now was, should I make a quick dash for the vicarage, or run back to my friends? As I stood weighing up my options, I froze to the spot as I saw the dark figure moving towards me. As he drew closer, he lifted his hand in a friendly wave; I became quite calm, I knew that wave - it was John, he was home. I hurried towards him, I could see the lights of the vicarage behind him, John had arrived home early.

Suddenly his arms were around me. 'Mary! You're shaking, what's wrong?'

'Nothing, John, nothing ... not now, I was being silly. I could not make out who was stood by the open grave.'

'Mary, I'm so sorry, I came out to meet you because I was worried about the grave that Bill dug this morning. I couldn't remember if he had roped it off; I knew you would walk back this way from Jane's, so I left London early - but I didn't mean to frighten you.'

'I'm all right, John, I was just being very silly. How did it go in London?'

'No trouble, we have the money. Tomorrow I'll ring the contractors and they can start the job as soon as they like.'

'Oh John, that's wonderful, now how about supper?'

'Mary, you read my mind.'

I turned to take one last look at the church, the shadows still looked sinister - I could still feel a strange atmosphere. Well I didn't care, my husband was home.

As we moved towards the vicarage, we could hear the shrill ring of the telephone. We ran the last few yards to the front door - I was in such a hurry, I dropped my keys in the porch and before I could pick them up, John had his key already in the lock. I ran to the phone leaving John to pick up my keys. As I picked up the phone I was surprised to hear Ashley's voice on the other end. Ashley was John's very best friend; he was best man at our wedding, a huge, blond-haired man, he looked just like a Viking king.

As I visualised him on the other end of the phone, Ashley was speaking. 'Mary, it's John ...'

'Yes Ashley, he's here - he came home early. Do you want to speak to him?' I turned to the front door, the door was still wide open but no sign of John - just his keys hanging in the lock.

'Mary, what are you talking about ... ?'

'I thought you wanted to speak to John.'

'Mary, be quiet and listen, this is urgent. I want you to stay quite calm and sit down …'

'Ashley, I don't want to sit down, I want to know what you want, you are beginning to worry me.'

'Mary, there's been an accident …'

'An accident!'

'Please Mary, just listen! John's car was involved with another car not far from the hospital; I got to him in minutes but it's not good Mary, I need you here now. I have sent a car for you, it should be arriving at any moment.'

'It's here now Ashley, I can hear it coming up the drive. But I still don't understand …'

'Mary, you have no time, John needs you here now.'

The line went dead. I put the phone down and turned to the front door. As I left the house, I took John's keys from the door; I smiled as I put them in my pocket. John's key ring had a small photograph of our wedding. I couldn't see my keys anywhere, they were nowhere in the porch. I would have to use John's. I turned the double lock and slipped the keys into my pocket.

I climbed into the waiting car, said 'Hello' to the driver whom I had met before. I tried to sound calm but my heart was pounding. All the way to the hospital I kept thinking to myself, *what is going on, how could I have seen John and held him in my arms?* Yet Ashley had just told me that John was at the hospital.

The journey flashed by, I was at the hospital. Ashley was there to meet me, good and dependable as ever. We were in the lift and up to the floor where John was, very quickly. As we walked the long corridor to the special unit, I was thinking, *I don't want to look, it's not true,* but there he was lying motionless, wired up to many machines.

'Ashley, I can't.'

'You can Mary, John needs you, he's in a deep coma.'

'How can I help?'

'Just take John's hand and talk to him.'

'If he's in a coma, how will that help, will he be able to hear me?'

'We don't know how much anyone in a coma can hear, but we always hope.'

'But Ashley …'

'Please Mary, just do as I ask. I do have to leave you, I have another urgent case to see.'

I took the chair that Ashley offered me, sat down and took John's hand in mine. I prayed hard for help. I must have fallen asleep, because when I opened my eyes it was daylight. I still had John's hand in mine. As I sat looking at him, he opened his eyes, smiled and opened his right hand which had been tightly clenched and there were my keys - the keys he had picked up from the porch.

'Take them,' he said.

I took the keys and ran to the door shouting for Ashley. He came running along the corridor.

'What is it Mary, what's wrong!'

'John is awake, Ashley, he opened his eyes, he spoke to me.'

Ashley moved quickly to John's side, took John's wrist and gently took his pulse, then he turned to me and said, 'I'm sorry Mary, there is no change.'

'But Ashley, he opened his eyes.'

'No Mary ... you were still asleep. I looked in earlier and you were dead to the world. Go home and get some rest.'

'But I don't want to go home, Ashley.' I wanted to explain about the keys in John's hand but I changed my mind.

'Well if you won't go home, Mary, let me find you a room in the hospital where you can rest and be close to John.' Ashley showed me to a room and someone was sent to get some things I needed from home to be able to stay and be close to John.

I slept or tried to sleep in that room for four long weeks. Then, like a miracle, the day came when John opened his eyes and began to talk. He had no idea he had been in a coma for so long. When we explained what had happened, he kept apologising to me.

'It was my fault, Mary, I couldn't help it. Suddenly at the meeting, in the middle of negotiating for the boiler money, I thought of the open grave. Had Bill roped it off? Then I thought of you coming home from Jane's in the dark; would you see the open grave? I left the meeting early, driving much too fast. I arrived back in town in record time. As I passed the hospital, I tried to brake as a car crossed my path; that's when I hit the tree.'

'Please John, all is well now.' I wondered if I should tell him about the keys but decided I would tell him later - this was our secret.

I don't pretend to understand what had happened but I knew when John came home, he would. I only knew that our love was so strong that he had been with me in the churchyard. Now it was time for John to rest; I thanked Ashley for all he had done.

He just smiled and said, 'Mary, I'm so happy that my two very best friends are safely back together.'

In two weeks we were back home. John grew stronger every day; we were soon out walking. I still hadn't told him about the keys and the meeting that night. Then, as we were walking through the churchyard, John turned to me and said, 'Mary, when I was in a coma, I had the strangest dream ...'

I smiled and said, 'I know all about it.'

John said, 'I had a feeling you might.'

I knew I would never forget that night but we never spoke about it ever again.

Flame Of Hope

Clive Cornwall

As she stood washing up the breakfast things, she looked out upon the tiny plot she called the garden. Two or three ordinary birds were at the bird table. Turning away she wiped her hands on the corner of the tea towel before hanging it on the rail. Going into the hall she picked up the telephone and rang for the usual taxi to the usual destination. Turning off the radio, she then put on her red coat. Locking the front door she waited for the taxi which arrived in a few minutes.

It was a dull, damp morning with little sense of life. On the way the taxi stopped at the supermarket, something that had become routine. It was the usual half a dozen items and then back into the taxi. The journey took longer than usual because of road works. Weaving across town and beyond she sat letting her mind wander over all sorts of things. She became slightly restless when she found herself reflecting on the fact that there did not seem to be a pattern in the world anymore. People weren't trustworthy. No social order. The old familiar patterns all gone. There was a time when you knew exactly what was what. Oh dear, she must be getting old! Ah well, she had her routine. She looked from the window as scenes passed before her eyes. She was aware of an old man being helped to his feet. Blue lights. Blue lights everywhere. Suddenly the world was frantic.

Not long afterwards they arrived at the usual destination. 'Shall I wait as usual?' asked the driver.

'Yes please,' she replied.

She got out and walked a distance into the clearing. Two or three grey squirrels bounced across the grass and up the nearest trees. She started to run and reaching him she threw her arms around him or at least, as far as she could get them. She hugged him tight. He was much older than she was by, perhaps, two or three hundred years. She always referred to the great oak as *him or he*. She hugged him for some time before leaving. Strength built up she returned home.

Candles glowed in various colours as she began to meditate. She was both seeking her 'inner self' and peace. She knew that from the acorn grew the great oak.

Seen Through A Window

Rita Eyrl

Monday, September 14th

I've just finished my breakfast and drank my usual two cups of tea. I'm now sitting at my window in my armchair to view the morning's events.

9.08am

Today is different. Jane's husband Tom hasn't gone to work. That's unusual. Now I wonder, will Mr X turn up? Tom goes out at 8.30, then Mr X arrives about 9.30 and stays a couple of hours. All I want to know is, who is Mr X and why is he visiting Jane? It's not that I'm a nosy person, I just take my neighbourhood watch duties seriously.

9.12am

There's Sandra from number twelve just crossing the road. Here comes Jenny, I might have known she wouldn't be far behind. Sometimes I think they are joined at the hip. For goodness sake you two, don't stand talking in front of Jane's house, you'll block my view.

9.18am

Now look, someone else has joined them, haven't seen her before. She looks a pretty girl, must be aged about 20. Blast it! If there's one thing I enjoy it's a good fight and I'll miss it if they stand there talking. If Jane is having an affair with Mr X and he turns up now, Tom will find out and then there'll be trouble. What time is it now?

9.25am

Crikey, five minutes to go. I'm getting quite tense now. Have I got time to put the kettle on? I'm feeling a little thirsty. No, I'd miss Mr X arriving. Mr Brown is slowly walking up with the aid of two sticks, poor chap arthritis can be so debilitating. Thank goodness, the group's moved to let him pass and now they are dispersing.

9.30am

I don't believe it, the telephone is ringing. I can't stand not answering it. Stick it out girl, to answer the phone I'd have to go into the hall and I'd miss the action.

9.32am

Just as well I didn't move, here's Mr X now. I must say he's a bit of a stunner! Tall, dark, handsome, with a moustache. He's going into Jane's house; nothing happening yet.

9.45am

What's this? They are all coming out of the house laughing together. Maybe they are all swingers, although I wouldn't have thought Tom and Jane were the type.

9.47am

Blimey, Jane's coming across the road to my house with a note in her hand. Thank heaven I've got net curtains so I can't be seen. 'Buster, fetch the note, here boy, good dog.' Let's see, what's it say?

Dear Alice, rang you earlier, was hoping you could join us. We're visiting a country park today and then having lunch. My brother Mark is over from New Zealand for three months. He's staying at a nearby hotel, but visits me every day.

Sorry to have missed you.

Love Jane.

Well, I now know who Mr X is, and why he's visiting Jane. Pity I didn't answer the phone.

When The Straw Man Comes A-Calling

Simon Wright

A storm was blowing. Old man Johnston was fussing, concerned at the prospect of slates coming off his roof. The younger man was worried too. He kept glancing out the window to make sure his new sports car was okay. His wife, the old man's daughter, assured him he needn't worry. Her irritation showed. It had been difficult getting the kids to bed. They were so excited. Their hyperactive behaviour had been driving her to distraction. Her husband and father had, of course, been too preoccupied to help. Now, in-between sups of wine, she was packing presents into stockings, one of which was labelled 'Jack', the other 'Jennifer'.

Though they had been sent to their bedroom a whole hour earlier, seven-year-old Jack and his older sister Jennifer were far from asleep. Having fooled their mother into thinking they were safely tucked up, they had jumped out of bed and climbed up onto the window sill to keep watch. Jennifer had a small torch which she was shining out the window. She hoped it would illuminate tonight's eagerly anticipated visitor.

'Will you stop peering out of that window every five minutes,' snapped Mary, her patience stretched to breaking point. 'Nothing's going to happen and even if it does, you'll be covered by the insurance.'

'I thought I heard something,' countered her husband.

'Probably another of my tiles flying off,' moaned her father.

'Do you think my car's far enough away from the roof?' continued the younger man, glancing out through the curtains again. 'Maybe I should move it?'

His wife sighed, 'Where exactly are you going to move it John? You've parked it as far away from the dratted trees as possible. If you move it away from the house, it'll only be nearer the trees!'

'I could park it up by the road?'

'But to do that, you'd have to drive it right between all those trees you're so worried about and then, even worse, you'd have to walk all the way back in the wind and the rain and the darkness, avoiding getting hit by fallen branches, not to mention Dad's Houdini tiles!'

The sound of hooves on the driveway were lost in the wind. Cold breath spiralled into the night air from the nostrils of two sturdy horses, behind which rattled a heavily laden cart. At its front sat a figure dressed in red. He had a cape pulled down obscuring his face and held the reins comfortably in one hand. Nearing the house, his eyes were drawn to a light on the first floor. Kids faces were behind the light for just a second and then they were gone.

Upstairs the kids gasped. The moon had emerged from the cloud cover and they'd caught a glimpse of something. It was him! He was here! They both jumped down from their vantage point, fearing that he would see them. After all, little girls and boys were supposed to be asleep when he came a-calling, otherwise there would be no presents. Everyone knew that! Jennifer turned off her torch. They couldn't bring themselves to return to their beds though and instead peered over the window sill, out into the night. The moon had been obscured once more and for all their efforts, they could see nothing. Adults in the same position might have pondered whether what they had seen had been a trick of their imagination. Kids however suffer from no such delusions. They had seen him and he was coming!

The horses, their cart and master navigated the final part of the driveway. They came to a stop at the point where the narrow driveway widened into the tarmac covered area in front of the house. With a flick of his wrist upon the reins the cart's driver motioned the horses forward once again.

This time there was no mistaking the strange noise and it was Mary's turn to pull back the curtains. Whatever she expected to see, it certainly wasn't a horse-drawn cart! Her husband, having joined her at the window, was speechless. He looked across as if expecting her to have an answer. 'Dad, do you know anyone who has a horse-drawn cart around here?'

'Horse-drawn cart?' wheezed her father. 'Not since I was knee-high to a grasshopper!'

Peering over the rim of his spectacles, he too stared out the window into the gloom in disbelief. Their three faces were framed in the window as the red-cloaked figure slowly dismounted from the far side of the cart.

'A tinker?' suggested John.

'Don't really get them around here,' his father-in-law muttered.

'Wonder what he wants?' added John.

'Well, the only way we're going to find out is if we ask him!' replied his wife, ever the pragmatist.

'But he could be anyone, a thief or a mugger!' cautioned her husband.

'In a horse-drawn cart! We might be out in the wilds John, but we're not that backward.'

Neither of the men said anything, so she walked through to the hallway and began to unlock the door. The two men followed her, standing a little way behind.

Above, in the upstairs bedroom, the children now caught a better glimpse of the stranger. Jennifer was sure she saw him smile up at them, but she didn't feel like smiling back. They had been caught out. Caught awake on Christmas Eve! He had seen them, but he had not been the he that they'd been expecting! 'So this is what happens when children don't go to sleep,' she sobbed as she slid down the wall, back out of sight. Jack however stayed standing, staring transfixed out the window. A scream of warning was on his lips, but he was unable to voice it.

The woman's hand undid the last latch and moved to the door handle. Slowly she turned it and pulled the door open. It was dark outside, but the light above the front door came on. The glare from it blinded them to the sight of the approaching visitor, but not to the stink - he smelt awful! A sense of trepidation came over the three adults. Then, as the tall figure emerged through the doorway, they finally saw him clearly in the light.

This was no man that loomed before them, though a man's shape he had. He was nothing that they had ever seen or dreamt about, he was the stuff of nightmares. His body seemed to be made of straw; most of it covered by his tatty, blood-red cloak. The cloak was too short to cover all of his legs and arms which were unnaturally long in comparison to his torso. Rats clambered about his body and scuttled alongside him, and closer inspection revealed that the straw of his body was interlaced with manure.

The sensible thing would have been to have slammed the door in the face of this hideous apparition. Sense however flies out the window when horror sets in. The woman and the two men stood frozen with fright as the creature advanced upon them. Having entered the hallway, it brushed past them and set down a carefully wrapped parcel underneath the Christmas tree. Then, turning around, it leered a crooked smile and without saying a word headed back into the night.

The following afternoon the local priest came, paying his customary visit. His family and their family went back a long way and he knew that old mister Johnston found this time of year difficult now that his dear wife was no longer with them. This year however, Father O'Brien had called around rather earlier than usual. The Johnstons hadn't been in church which was unusual as they were regular churchgoers and never missed a Christmas service. His nagging fear that all was not well grew as he approached the house and spied the front door hanging wide open. He passed the silver sports car, standing immaculate and untouched, and entered the house calling out a tentative greeting. Inside, all was quiet, even the clocks on the wall seemed to have fallen silent. He noticed the Christmas presents lying untouched under the festively festooned tree including one neatly wrapped, but rather odd-looking parcel. What was odd about it was that the packaging was black, not very seasonal and it had no greetings card attached to identify who it was from or to. Still, Father O'Brien didn't think too much about it.

He checked the downstairs rooms and then made his way cautiously up the stairs. Mister Johnston was an extremely security-conscious man, not the sort to just forget to lock up. The priest feared that someone in the family had been struck down by illness and that they had rushed off to hospital. But this didn't stack up as the car was sitting in the driveway. Calling out their names again, he approached the first bedroom and, knocking on the door, slowly pushed it open. The bed was empty. Next, he entered the second bedroom. It was the same story. Mary's handbag lay beside the double bed. Again, if they were going somewhere, even in a rush, surely she would have brought her handbag with her? Finally, he went to the children's bedroom, though by now not expecting to find anything. He knocked twice and then pushed the door open. The room was a mess, strewn with toys. Father O'Brien chuckled. The room reminded him of his own nieces and nephews and the running battles their parents had with them to keep their rooms tidy. Nothing seemed particularly out of place, the bed sheets were crumpled and lying open, the curtain was half open, a torch lay on the floor by the window. The priest turned around and walked back down the stairs. As he did so, he pulled a mobile phone out from the recesses of his robe and dialled 999. 'There's probably a totally logical explanation, but better to be on the safe side.'

The old man, the husband, wife and their two kids were never seen again. Rumours abounded, but none could be substantiated. The local police undertook a thorough examination but found nothing of particular significance. The rectangular shaped black parcel turned out to be an old-looking book. Its covers were made of leather and its pages were brown with age. The writing was old fashioned, all thys and thous. It was illustrated with pictures.

The contents of the house fell into the possession of the old man's brother. Having little space for additional belongings and no wish to move from his city abode, he sold the house and decided to auction off most of the heirlooms. He took possession of many of his brother's treasure trove of books, kept some of them, sold or gave the rest away. The mysterious, old, leather-bound book, he sold to a book shop which in turn sold it on within a few weeks.

The book found its way onto a shelf on the landing of an old house, where a couple of children picked it up. The wording, though old fashioned, was written very clearly in big letters and the kids were fascinated by the illustrated pictures.

The opening words contrasted with the style of much of the chapters and read as follows:

When the straw man comes a-calling don't you be at the door for if he catches you in his gaze you will be no more.

The first picture showed three adults framed in an open doorway, a look of terror etched on their faces. There was a young woman and behind her, on either side, a young man and an older man.

The second photo showed two kids. Again, they were both staring straight ahead, transfixed. They were staring out of a window. An observant eye might have noticed the torch in the girl's hand. A questioning mind might have wondered what a torch was doing in a book that was over a hundred years old!

THE RAMBLE ACROSS THE MOORS

Raymond Thomas Edwards

The green and yellow minibus pulled into the roadside lay-by stopping by the kerb with an abrupt jerk. The driver rose from his seat, walked across the gangway, opened the bus' sliding door and stepped down onto the road. 'OK folks, this is it. I hope you have all brought your weatherproofs?' he said sarcastically eyeing up his passengers on the bus.

A voice piped up from the back of the bus, 'What do you need waterproofs for? Look at the sky, there isn't a cloud in sight.'

The driver then emphasised his last statement. 'It's my place to make sure you all have the right attire for your ramble, now I will repeat the question again, is there anyone who has not got weatherproof clothing?' No one answered his last request. 'OK then, make your way down the gangway and onto the road.' The driver pointed to a narrow pathway leading down a steep tree-lined gully. 'Now the pathway across the moors to Elkschurch has been clearly signposted with those little brown stumps, with a round red and yellow disc on, they are spaced approximately fifty yards apart. Whatever you do, keep to the paths and don't wander off alone. I can't stress this point enough, just follow the signposts. The walk to Elkschurch as the crow flies is about 10 miles. The time is now 8.30am, giving you plenty of time for a nice leisurely walk in the fresh air. Approximately 6 miles from this point the trail leads into a beautiful, secluded valley were an old stone bridge fords a small, fast-flowing stream. There are facilities here like toilets, tables and benches to sit on and enjoy your well-earned rest to have your sandwiches and drinks. Also waste bins have been provided for your rubbish, so will you please use them. Now it is a steep climb out of this valley, you are then on an open, desolate, windswept moor, with no shelter whatsoever. The path twists and turns like a snake, but I must emphasise this once again, keep to the pathways and follow the signs, it's about 4 miles to Elkschurch from there. I will pick you up outside the village pub, *The Dog and Duck* at 6 o'clock tonight. If you do happen to arrive there early and feel like refreshments there's a nice little cafe come tourist shop in the village.'

Watching all his charges slowly walking down the narrow path to start their 10 mile ramble across the moors, he waved to them and shouted in a sarcastic voice, 'And don't get lost.'

The rambling party was a mixed assortment of people and consisted of a father and son, two old spinster ladies, two old gentlemen, a husband and wife. These older members of the party were all around the same age and all supporting proudly on their coats a rambler's badge. So it would appear they all belonged to the same ramblers' club and were charting unknown territories. For they all seemed very excited of their prospects of walking across the moors. And last, but not least, two young girl students. The two girls spoke with a strong French accent, but looking at the way they were dressed had all the right equipment to stay alive and survive on those cold, desolate moors.

The father and son team on the other hand were the least prepared for the ramble. It looked as though everything had been hastily thrown into their rucksacks. Where the rest of the party wore stout walking boots, these two were decked out in trainers. Their rucksacks seemed to have been filled with flimsy, cheap items, blue plastic weatherproofs, the kind you would buy from your local market. But looking up into that clear blue sky there was hardly a breeze blowing, the sun was now making its power known, as members of the party were taking off the heavier garments, as the beads of sweat truckled down their faces.

Navigating themselves along the narrow pathways, occasionally checking their maps and ticking off certain pencilled-in map references they had made. Each side of them, rock faces rose up from the earth all covered in pretty flowers of all sizes and descriptions. Purple heather and yellow gorse bushes all added to the panoramic beauty of the area. A nice, steady leisurely walk, stopping now and then to take in the beauty of the scenery and take a few snapshots to record the points of interest on their ramble.

They finally arrived at a stone bridge spanning a small fast-flowing stream in a picturesque secluded valley, just as the driver had described to them. Where, they at once downed their knapsacks and sat down for a well-earned rest. The walk itself hadn't been too arduous, but the power of the sun had increased making breathing very difficult. The younger ones just slumped down on the ground and just lay there relaxing. Cool drinks were the main thing on the agenda as the members of the rambling party panted and gulped down those precious drops of liquid.

After quenching that dryness in their throats their sandwiches tasted like a four course banquet. It was now midday, the father and son couple among the ramblers had been arguing continuously since leaving the bus at the lay-by. David was the youngest son of John and Pamela Cole. He was twenty-years-old and through his constant studying had won himself a place at university where he had been attending for the past two years. He still had a long way to go with his studies to get his final diploma and his masters degree, when one night he'd delivered a bombshell to his family in the way of a message that said, *I've fallen head over heels in love with a girl I have met recently and I'm leaving university to set up home with her.* The very text of the message horrified his family. He had spent all those years studying for a degree, only to throw it all away on a whim. A meeting was hurriedly set up with the members of the family to decide what course of action to take. It was decided to draw straws, the loser being the one to sort out the youngster's problems and talk some sense into him. This was easier said than done, for the boy was very headstrong, so whoever had the short straw was in for a job and a half. Each one in turn had picked out a straw then drawn a deep breath and passed on the straws to the next one.

His father ended up with the short straw, and made it very clear he did not relish the idea of trying to convince his young son to go back to university. He knew only too well the task that lay ahead of him wouldn't be easy and the last thing he wanted to do was to upset his son. He knew from experience he had to choose the right words and tactfully use them, if he was to gain any headway at all. So he'd decided to pick a neutral ground and seeing this ramble advertised in the local paper thought it would be the ideal place, but on reaching the bridge he knew that he was fighting a losing battle. His manoeuvring and trying to pick the correct words to outline his argument had all been in vain. His son had made his mind up and no amount of talking would make him change it. So deciding to leave his son to his own devices he chose to mingle and chat to the rest of the rambling party.

His first encounter was with the two old spinster ladies who jokingly remarked they had noticed he was having difficulty in getting his point across to his son. John explained the reason for the ramble and told them about his drawing the short straw. They were both very sympathetic as they listened intently to his story before giving their comments. One pointed out the fact the only way to experience life is to live by your mistakes, sometimes your heart rules your head. The only way forward is to let nature take its course.

Leaving the old ladies with their views in his mind he then got in conversation with two old men and the man and wife, discussing the finer points of that day's ramble. The last couple he spoke to were the two young French students. Spending a large amount of his time in France in his younger days he could speak their language fluently. This was a big asset because he could speak better French than they could English and being able to relive his time there and the places he had visited made the two girls bubble with enthusiasm as he explained in their own language his experiences.

Leaving the girls to relax and enjoy their well-earned rest, he couldn't relax himself, it was as though a sixth sense was tugging at his mind, he could sense danger. He decided to go for a short walk along the small, winding stream and perhaps clear his head. He noticed the colour of the water was beginning to change to a tinted brown. *That's funny,* he thought to himself, *that could only mean one thing, rain!* But looking up it was like being in a large bucket, you were limited as to how far you could see. The sky was lovely and blue in this beautiful green valley. He had a funny feeling in the pit of his stomach and he just couldn't settle and relax like the rest.

His son by this time was also stretched out on the grass soaking up the sun. He made an excuse to his son about not being tired and decided to climb up the steep path out of the valley to see if he could see their final destination. Climbing up the steep path made him puff and pant with the sun's rays beating down on him relentlessly. On reaching the top and peering across the open moors, he felt his blood turn to ice, for in the distance, the sky was as black as coal. He could see the forked lightning striking the ground, he could feel the wind pressure building up and lashing his face like a whip. A storm was bearing down on them fast, he felt shivers down his spine as he caught the cold draught from the oncoming rain. How long would it take to turn that little stream in the valley below into a raging torrent and trap the ramblers, and there was the possibility of someone being drowned in this deluge?

His first thoughts were to warn the rest, but his shouting was of no avail. They were all sleeping like babies, all oblivious of the danger that threatened them, having their afternoon siesta. He had no choice, he had to climb back down and warn them. But this task was easier said than done. The sun's heat had drained them, like a battery going flat and all they wanted to do was rest. He had one more trick up his sleeve, he had to get them up onto their feet and out of this valley. He was now shouting at them at the top of his voice, 'There's a terrible storm coming straight at us, if we don't hurry we shall all be drowned in this valley. If you don't believe me take a look at the stream, when we arrived here an hour ago the stream's water was as clear as crystal, come and take a look at it now.'

Getting lazily to their feet they mumbled amongst themselves, 'Anything for a quiet life.' The sun was still shining out of a clear blue sky as they made their way to the banks of the stream. The sight that met their eyes started the panic buttons ringing, for where once flowed a stream of clear water, it had now turned to a muddy brown and was increasing in size and volume fast. They hadn't a moment to lose, as they hurriedly prepared themselves for the oncoming storm. Looking up, they still couldn't believe what was happening to them. The sky was still a clear blue. Getting themselves organised they began their ascent up the steep path out of the valley leading to the top. Looking out across the desolate moors, the storm clouds were almost upon them. They could feel the ferocity of the wind and rain whiplashing them as it bore down on them relentlessly. This was the mother of all storms and if they were to survive it they needed a plan.

Looking back down into the valley where they had all been resting only a few moments ago, the complete area was awash with dark brown muddy water. Thanking their lucky stars, they apologised to David's father for doubting him, if it hadn't been for his quick thinking they could be down there in that lot. They at once began organising themselves trying to find the best way to tackle the oncoming storm, for the moors were bleak and desolate and there was nowhere to shelter.

John made a simple suggestion that seemed to make a great deal of sense. 'Instead of trying to fight the storm by ourselves, what it needs is a team effort.' He then began outlining his simple plan to help save all their lives. 'When geese fly in formation, the lead goose takes the brunt of the wind so causing an air stream and providing the rest of the flock with a slipstream to fly in. If we all walk with our hands on the person in front and that way push our way through the storm. Then at regular intervals keep changing places with the person in the front to give him a rest.' They all agreed to the proposed plan and set off to face the merciless gale force wind and rain that was battering them. It was like being whipped with a thousand razor-sharp whips, the fury of the storm lashing them. The band of ramblers with their hands on the person in front began pushing their way through the storm. It was no time to be faint-hearted if they wanted to live they had to battle their way through it, which by now was right on top of them.

It was as dark as night as they began navigating themselves along the narrow pathways. Water was gushing all around them, making the paths like trails of mud. Debris was being tossed around by the wind, it was as though every step forward they took they were blown back two, but the grim determination to survive gave them that extra strength. They began inching their way forward down the twisting, winding paths following the beacons in the night, the wooden signposts leading them back to safety. The going was tougher than they anticipated, all completely exhausted from their ordeal they couldn't walk another step.

The hostile, weather-beaten moor looked very inhospitable as their eyes scanned for even the smallest obstacles to shelter behind, but alas, there was none. So all decided to hug together to keep out the elements; when they saw torch lights farther down the trail and they could hear voices, there was still another mile and a half to go.

The coach driver seeing the storm had raised the alarm and a rescue team had been sent out to find the ramblers. On seeing the pathetic sight of the ten ramblers they at once began making a make-shift tent with plastic sheets they had brought with them where they could huddle together and take shelter and weather the storm.

The storm finally died out leaving a sky full of twinkling stars. By this time more rescuers had arrived to take the ramblers off the moor and to safety. A day full of sunshine and promise with a nice leisurely ramble across the moors enjoying all that nature has to offer had turned out to be one of life's worst nightmares. Having all rested up at the local rescue centre and been given a medical for possible ailments, they had all been given the stamp of approval, so it was safe to continue their return journey home.

The coach driver walked down the gangway of the minibus and as he spoke his voice was full of emotion. 'You had me worried sick,' he said. 'I was driving back to Elkschurch to pick you up when I saw the sky in the distance suddenly turn black. I turned on the radio and it said a storm had developed out in the Channel and it had suddenly changed direction, picked up speed and was heading inland at an alarming rate, warning people to stay indoors. I at once telephoned the moors rescue team. One thing about this escapade it will be something to tell your grandchildren about.' He then returned to his seat, 'Right folks we have all had enough excitement for one day, home sweet home, here we come,' he said with a sigh of relief.

At that the ramblers began singing, 'For he's a jolly good fellow, for he's a jolly good fellow.'

The coach driver, overcome with emotion, had difficulty in holding the tears back.

David was sitting next to his father and twitching nervously, 'Dad,' he said slowly, 'In the past few hours I've been thinking a lot, you did a very courageous thing coming back down that path to warn us, then most of us wouldn't believe you, but it takes guts sometimes to admit the truth to someone. You're right about my future, I have been very selfish on my outlook on life, it takes something like this to make you stop and count your blessings. I have decided to make you and Mom proud of me by getting my diploma. I'm going back to university to finish my exams.'

His father with a tear trickling down his face grasped his son's hand. 'Your studies won't last forever, there's no reason why your relationship with your young lady should not continue, but it's always best in life to have some diplomas under your belt to enable you to get a better job.'

One of the old spinster ladies sitting behind John tapped him on the shoulder. 'What did I tell you down by that stone bridge a few hours ago, let nature take its course.'

He turned around and smiled at her, 'If it takes a raging storm to decide one's destiny, so be it.'

On Lucerna Moor
K Hale

His hair was a stormy sea, tousled and ruffled up, forming messy waves and untidy troughs around his gaunt, pale face. Wearily, he trudged onwards through the cold, windy night, his head buried in his torn and ragged coat against the gale. Looking up for but a second, he caught sight of a gloomy barn in the distance. He smiled grimly. He would rest there tonight, away from the wind, away from the rain, but above all, away from his thoughts of the darkness. He knew he had to reach the barn, his flickering spark of hope, before the black tide at the edge of his troubled brain flowed inwards to engulf him in the murky gloom of his depression. Dwelling on his deepest miseries, feeling his eyes smart at the biting wind and bitterly aware of the perishing rain's teeth piercing his cold skin, he caught his foot in a tangle of thorns. He stumbled, dreading to see what he knew he could not avoid - the candles in the marsh.

Arabella Millbarn, daughter of the well-known farmer, Angus Millbarn, and the late Mrs Maria Millbarn, sat up. She had been sleeping soundly, but something had woken her. Rubbing her eyes she pulled back the heavy, fading blue curtains at her window to look out across the dark marshes of Lucerna Moor and watched as the barn owls swooped silently around the farm buildings. Yawning widely, she reached out and carefully lit a candle. Shivering slightly against the autumn cold, Arabella got quietly out of bed and crept down the creaky farmhouse stairs, her short, beige night-dress tight around her skinny white legs. Slowly she opened the oak door and peered out into the starry night. As she crossed the cobbled, horse-smelling yard, she blew out the candle because the moon gave her sufficient light to see by.

'Humbug!'

A border collie ran to her heels, silent like his mistress. He was Arabella's only friend and had been since she was eight, when her mother had first become ill, six desperate years ago. She bent down and patted his thick fur. Stepping lightly on the wet cobbles, the subdued pair made their way to the dim outline of the barn. The door creaked as Arabella opened it stealthily, and the thin beam of white moonlight crept across the stone floor. She ran to the sweet-smelling bales of hay, her black, hurriedly laced-up boots barely touching the ground. She climbed laboriously up the haystack, a patient Humbug under her arm, so, upon reaching the top of her soft bed of hay, instinctively lay down. Sleep gripped her almost at once, but she was then dropped into the drowning clasp of the nightmare.

For the second time that cloudless night, Arabella awoke. For the second time, it was the nightmare that had awoken her. She had been experiencing the nightmare more and more frequently since the tragic day when Maria Millbarn had breathed her last and given up her ghost to the heavens.

Arabella held Humbug to her body. Of course, she told herself, it was merely a dream, and there hadn't been a barn on Lucerna Moor for almost a thousand years, except for the one she was in. Unable to suppress a shiver, she glanced around the only barn on Lucerna Moor. Humbug began to stare upwards towards the beams, which creaked and groaned. *Due to the wind,* thought Arabella, but it was a still night. Humbug continued to stare up into the darkness. Suddenly, his nose began to twitch, he began to whine pitifully and his ears drooped. Before Arabella could make any move to stop him, he jumped from the musty hay, to land on the muddy, uneven stone flags. He nosed open the door, before running out across the yard. The splintering door creaked shut, leaving Arabella alone in the smothering darkness. Slowly, with her back prickling, she crept down the pile of withered hay, her shaky breath drawing in its stale smell. She crept stealthily across the cold, bare ground and out into the perishing night.

Arabella was cold, although the icy temperature of the night was only skin deep. But she felt a tugging chill, gripping at her heart. *Well,* she thought nervously, *it was a cold night.*

'Humbug? Humbug?' she hissed.

He did not appear. He may not have heard ... an echoing bang made her jump. She turned uneasily, vividly remembering the pressing fear and passion of the nightmare and saw - the gate. It was an ordinary gate - nothing more, nothing less, but although there was no wind, it was swinging back and forth on its hinges, as though controlled by a supernatural force. However, Arabella told herself meekly, there were no such forces. Silently, the tiny hairs on the back of her neck prickling, she set off through the gate, now still, and began to search out on the deserted marshes of Lucerna Moor.

'Humbug?' Arabella's voice began to quiver. 'Humbug?'

Just visible out of the very corner of her eye, Arabella could see the faint glimmer of light. It flickered, like the flame of a candle brushed by a breeze. It began to grow slowly clearer as others like it began to ignite, and Arabella saw that they shimmered, as though she was seeing them through a haze. Tremulously, she clasped her necklace, which was all she had left of her mother. It wasn't valuable, but to Arabella, nothing could be as precious. It was a simple leather thong, dyed black, with three red glass beads; one for the body, one for the mind and one for the spirit. The third bead was cold, despite the warmth of Arabella's hands. She turned, suddenly, feeling someone brush at the back of her neck, where the clasp of the necklace lay. There, the barn seemed to loom, silhouetted against the night sky, and Arabella, vivid, horrifying memories from the nightmare dissolving into her troubled brain, turned and began to run. She ran from home and the safety of her own bed, drawn away by some mysterious magnet.

The lights! They were so much like the flickering candles of the nightmare, and Arabella knew that there would be no chance of waking, for now the nightmare was real, although all realities were turning on their heads.

If she fixed her eye on a light, then maybe - just maybe - she would be safe from the marsh. Again she felt the clutching breeze at the nape of her neck, like a cool pair of hands. A protruding snare of heather clutched at her foot and she fell. She seemed to be falling slowly and she became aware that there were tears in her eyes, and that her face was drenched with cold sweat. Then she saw them: the glimmering flames of the candles that lingered beneath the murky surface of the bog. Rising to meet her, the marsh enveloped and consumed her, and the black waves washed over her terrified senses.

The hand that had been so strongly gripping her lifeless wrist, released her and began stroking her forehead, whispering in her ear. Arabella began to murmur and, through a foggy curtain of unconsciousness, she saw the faint glimmering outline of a boy and felt his cool hands brushing at her neck. She was sure she recognised him, but she gave way to the dark once more, and when she awoke again, she was alone on the topmost bank overlooking Lucerna Moor. The candles had vanished and the sun's pink and orange rays broke out into the morning sky, as the silver stars of the night before vanished. She smiled as she felt for her necklace.

But it was gone.

John Riteholme had just returned from the mournful burial of Mrs Arabella Riteholme, formerly Arabella Millbarn. Dejectedly, he sat in a fading armchair, overlooking Lucerna Moor, where he often sat to watch the birds and other such wildlife. Today, however, he had little interest in birds and picked up the Daily News. *Mysterious Body Discovered In Marsh,* he read. The article described the body of a young boy, aged about fifteen. The body was thought to have been about nine hundred years old, although in his hand he clasped a necklace from a much later period.

John looked at the sketch of the item. It was a simple leather thong, dyed black, with three red glass beads.

You'll Never Know!

J W Whiteacre

The move to the Mill House went according to plan. At last Sally and James had achieved their aim to leave the city and live simple lives in the country. The removal men had gone and most of the household items were roughly in the correct rooms. They stood on the terrace and raised their glasses of wine to the sea and fields.

Attached to the house was the old mill shop and the derelict windmill was at the bottom of the garden path. 'I can just picture some jolly-faced miller leaning over the stable door, handing out sacks of flour to customers,' said Sal. 'It's all very romantic. We'll have supper on the terrace. No traffic, no noisy folk - just country sounds. Open another bottle of wine darling.'

The couple gazed out to sea. The breakwater light was flashing, highlighting the bodies of fishing boats as they bobbed around in the evening.

The first night passed gently into dawn. 'Fresh start! Come on Sal, wakey, wakey!' called James as he poured coffee. Sally arrived in her dressing gown. James opened the old shop door. A shaft of light almost blinded Sally and for a split second she thought she saw something fly through the shaft. Just for a moment she froze.

'I think I need lots of caffeine,' she muttered and swallowed a cupful in one go. She noticed a little smirk on her husband's face. Glancing back to the shop, she saw a piece of material resting on a trapdoor.

'Oh look,' said James. 'A miller's apron,' and hung it on a nail. Then he returned to making breakfast. Sally and James spent most of the day trying to transform the house into a home.

'Come on, let's have a walk round the garden Sal. We haven't really explored at all. It's nearly dark.' James took her hand and led her down the garden path. The breakwater light began flashing to summon dusk.

'Look James, there's the well in the corner. The borders are packed and can you see the grain? It must have escaped from the mill. There's wheat everywhere! There's a fountain - *ouch!* Something's just pulled out a piece of my hair! I'm bleeding! James ... James where are you?'

Sally ran down the path to the mill. 'Get me a towel James, I'm bleeding.' She disturbed all the roosting crows and the night became full of flapping and flying - straight at her face, pecking and flapping. 'If this is one of your jokes - it's sick! You're *sick!*'

As Sally tried to focus on the path to the house she saw a light flashing from the shop door. 'There you are, you idiot! You have gone back for a towel,' she cried as she began running up the path. The light from the doorway seemed to be sending a signal to the breakwater light. Rushing past the well, a giant claw grabbed her and the wheat suddenly grew taller and thicker, winding round her like a rope, lashing her against the fence. Sobbing and struggling to free herself, out of the corner of her eye Sally noticed the breakwater light had changed to green. A great wave surged up, travelling quickly towards her. There was just enough light to see an army of human legs with great crab-like claws for hands. Her screams echoed through the night and forced the owls to hoot and screech in opposition. 'I'm going to die!' she cried. She managed to escape. However, as she reached the house the wave turned into a slimy gel at her feet. The scene was horrific! Giant crab claws and parts of human legs sticking up everywhere in this solid wave of awfulness.

Beside herself with fear, Sally repeated her frantic calls for help, grabbing a towel to mop up the blood. Suddenly the owls, crows and sea all went deadly silent - as the windmill started turning. 'That's impossible, all the parts are missing. It hasn't turned for years. Please God, get me out of here!' Sally cried.

The night became cloudless. The moon shone down - showing bodies hanging from every tree - just swaying and snakes crawling in and out of arms and legs, out of pockets and round necks. At that moment Sally passed out.

As daylight drifted onto her face, Sally opened her eyes. Her blood curdled at the scene. All the crows from the mill were scattered on the floor - beheaded - blood everywhere - wings still flying without heads.

Revulsion set in as she crawled to the door for air. There she saw James, naked except for the miller's apron, drooped over the well. Sheer terror struck her heart.

In a city flat an alarm clock rang out loudly. 'Morning, thank goodness it's morning! I've had this awful nightmare darling! We're not buying that mill we viewed the other day. I had this terrible dream - James - James,' she put her arm to where he was lying beside her. 'Oh no, *no!*' Sally's arm landed in a slimy, messy pie! A crow, slimy pie! Loose wings flapped all over the duvet and headless birds chirped. Slowly Sally was sucked into the mixture, inch by inch - and was liquified.

At the mill house life couldn't be better. 'Let's drink to liquidation!' said James, looking at the stunning beauty lounging on the terrace. In the distance James saw a large van winding its way along the lanes. Just as lunch was about to be served, there was a loud knocking on the shop door. James, slightly irritated by the intrusion, answered the door.

'I'm your travelling grocery service, Sir. I used to be miller here, but now I deliver essential supplies for folk in remote parts. My name is Michael.'

'Hello Michael, I'm James and this is my-er-wife, Suzanna. I've recently taken early retirement to be with her.'

'Really,' said Michael.

'He's wonderfully talented,' boasted Suzanna. 'He created all the best stunts for big films.'

'Is that so?' said Michael. 'I'm quite good at the odd stunt myself!'

Suzanna scoffed. 'Oh, not like James. The best producers used him you know ... and he gave it all up for *me!* Isn't that sweet?' she kissed James on the cheek.

'Is that so?' smiled Michael. 'Are you short of anything?'

'We've brought oodles of goodies for our creature comforts but we'd better see what's on offer - just in case - just to be sociable. Hopefully lunch won't ruin. You're our first visitor.'

'Blue cheese darling. We forgot it. How will we cope? Spaghetti, we could do with extra. I suppose you'll tell me you make your own pasta from your home-grown wheat?' babbled Suzanna.

'Something like that,' grinned Michael.

Suddenly looking bored, Suzanna waved her hand. 'Pay the man. Lunch calls.' She grabbed the blue cheese.

'You've forgotten the spaghetti Madam.'

Michael handed it to James.

'Time for my own lunch now,' said the miller.

'You must be exhausted, driving that thing around all day,' James commented.

'Oh no, I don't drive and serve. My wonderful wife does the driving. Wave to these good folk my love!'

Suzanna and James suddenly lost their appetite. They froze on the spot - from the driver's wing mirror - there was Sally's face! She blew them a kiss and drove away with a jerk as Michael was closing the back doors. A large blue cheese bounced out. It quickly glowed a violent red and rolled towards the couple, gaining in size and speed. Suzanna's cheese throbbed, changing colour and exploded in her hand, splattering her face and arms. The burning sensation was unbearable. She began to scream. The spaghetti burst from the bag. It grew thick and long, changing into snakes with violent tongues, wrapping and lashing them together - stinging, biting. The exhaust let out a huge bang. Hot, molten liquid gushed out, sweeping them to the shop door. The shaft of light turned into a laser beam, burning a hole in the trapdoor. The liquid flushed the lovers downwards into a very warm hell. All Sally and Michael could hear were screams as they fell down and down.

'Nice one Sally!' laughed Michael. 'You're good at this! My disguise really fooled him. He didn't even recognise his own *brother!* What a stunt!'

Sally passed him lunch. 'I had a superb teacher. Who said it was a stunt? I did it for real this time.'

She glanced in her mirror to witness satisfied snakes, waving triumphant tongues, dripping red, slithering down the lane.

THE REAL TERROR
Guy Fletcher

He adored this place and I can quite see why. The wind is howling on dramatic Burry Holms and I imagine it to be his spirit cursing me. The sunset has turned the white feather clouds a blood-red as well as the sea. This is an awe-inspiring view.

It was a year ago today that my life changed forever. I had just returned from a business trip to Geneva and was sleeping late. Unfortunately my wife woke me and complained about a lack of money coming into the household. Considering that we lived in a large house in the country and had a BMW and a Porsche, I rather took offence.

'Bloody hell, read this Steve!' exclaimed Jayne, handing me the newspaper.

Brutal Revenge was the headline and the article explained how a man had been shot in the head, but only after writing a confession. He admitted bullying his killer at school and wrote about how much he regretted his actions. The interesting and worrying fact was that the man whom the police were searching for was none other than my wife's ex-husband.

Let me fill in some useful background information: Luke Jarvis was a quiet, reflective man who wrote elegant poetry in his spare time and was contented with his job as a librarian. He was quite different from Jayne but she undoubtedly loved him initially. The trouble with Jayne was that she was easily bored and to cut a long story short, she met me, a fellow materialist. I pretended to be his friend whilst *knocking off his wife,* to put it bluntly. He knew, but was so desperate to stay with Jayne that he said nothing, even when she left he just cried. There were no violent scenes, merely quiet despair. I'd have kicked the hell out of me personally but there we are.

That was ten or so years ago and now he had finally become angry. Beware the fury of a quiet man.

'The nutter will be coming after us next,' said Jayne.

Outside it was a dark, dank, gloomy November evening. The trees looked particularly sinister now and I locked all the doors with a sense of dread pervading my soul, although I endeavoured to remain calm.
'No, don't worry, the police will have got him by now, but why did he murder that bloke after all this time?'

'Good question. I'll answer if you like.' Jarvis had emerged from the dining room with a truly menacing glare and even more frighteningly, a long, sharp knife.

Words are inadequate to describe the sensation of terror I felt at that moment although it was also surreal, like watching a horror film but unfortunately I was one of the stars. Jayne started to scream and I held her closely.

'Sit down, shut up and I'll tell you a story,' continued Jarvis, more powerful now than he'd ever been. He was unshaven, dirty and his eyes were those of a fanatic. 'I haven't got long to live, terminal heart problem I'm afraid. Mind you it has given me the opportunity to settle a few scores. That bastard Barrett made my life hell at school and I used to puke every morning, even contemplating suicide. But the fear I caused him, the way he begged for mercy: it was scintillating. But I'm not here to talk about the tragic demise of Barrett, much as I'd like to, as he caused a mere fraction of the pain you two inflicted. Do you know how hard it is to see someone you love kissing another man, loving another man and knowing she has contempt for me when previously there was love? By the way, you might be interested in these my friends.' He reached inside his coat and threw an envelope onto the table. 'Open it and enjoy!' commanded Jarvis

With trembling hands, I opened the envelope and my fear evaporated like breath in the cold air and was replaced by anger, for in front of me were photographs of Jayne embracing and holding hands with another man.

'What are the lines from Othello?' said Jarvis, clearly enjoying the moment and still speaking in a soft but deadly tone. 'Look to her, Moor, if thou has eyes to see: she has deceived her father, and may thee.'

'You always did like your literature Luke,' I said.

'Yes, but enough of this. I'm going to let one of you live. Who should it be? State your cases.'

I was looking for an opportunity to rush Jarvis but it's not as easy as in the movies. 'I'm begging you Luke,' I announced. Now I felt a sadness for Luke and immense disappointment that Jayne had betrayed me. Bring it on, I was drained.

Jayne then pleaded with Jarvis, saying how she had made a terrible mistake leaving him and that he was the only man she had ever really loved. It was sickening and I really believed Jarvis and me empathised at this moment. Suddenly Jarvis cut both of Jayne's cheeks deeply with a knife. Time seemed to stop and then I was aware of Jarvis leaving with the following chilling words. 'Your beauty has gone now Jayne, that's the only thing you ever really had so it's worse than killing you.'

Inhuman screams emanated from Jayne as blood rushed from her awful wounds. My emotions were incredibly confused for I was glad to be alive but now no longer angry with Jayne for she was in such anguish. As for Jarvis, well he died from a massive heart attack some hours later, his revenge accomplished. It really was a dish served cold.

Jarvis did kill Jayne that night, a slow death that took over nine months. I didn't leave her but the bottle now became her lover as it has for countless others. After one particularly drunken session she stepped out onto a road, but never made it to the other side.

Real terror doesn't involve a demon invading your home. Horrific acts come from human beings, not usually from some mad stranger but from someone whom life has just pushed too far. Luke Jarvis then became a monster.

I have re-evaluated my life since that shocking night. I no longer have a passion for superficial materialism and Jarvis haunts my dreams. How callous we were towards him but how he made us pay. I feel partly possessed and that I am actually Jarvis looking out onto the wild, unforgiving ocean.

The blood-red has now disappeared from the Burry Holms sky and darkness begins to descend. It's time to go back to the hotel for alcohol and more reflection.

Disturbed

Sandra MacLean

He woke to a fluent tapping noise. His memory was quiet and it took him a second to recognise the sound was against glass. He looked over at his window. A black raven was sitting on his window sill watching him. It was motionless except for the glistening movement of its opaque eyes. As it stared at him he felt his world shifting; the air in front of him undulated and he closed his eyes to focus. He felt sick as if on water: his head enveloped a dull hangover. When he opened his eyes the raven was gone and the air around him had settled.

After showering and shaving in his usual Monday morning routine, Phil left his flat and commenced his daily walk to work. He turned the corner and stopped. There was a man standing across the road staring at him. He was smiling at Phil in recognition. There was no mistaking his cap. It was his grandfather. The raven was perched on his shoulder.

Phil panicked. His grandad had been dead three years. He squeezed his eyes shut and when he opened them again his grandad had gone. The raven stood on the wall; it blinked as it stared at him. Phil broke into a run and reached the corner where his morning café was. The place was called *Joe's* but it wasn't as he remembered it from Friday. The colour had changed. He pushed the door open and heaved a sigh of relief when he saw his favourite waitress behind the counter. He had a feeling there was something different about her too, but he couldn't isolate the source. He felt himself relax as she smiled over at him in recognition and reached for an espresso cup. A couple walked in behind him, holding hands.

As he sat in a booth he felt the strong rush of coffee, he felt his mind arriving from its morning holiday and sensibility returning. His brain resembled a frequently played jukebox whose discs were currently being returned to their allocated slots. He reasoned with himself that Sally, the waitress, had probably just changed her hair and the café had probably been given a lick of paint over the weekend. The guy who looked like his grandad had given him a shock, but then he remembered that we all supposedly have our doubles. Phil took his last sip of coffee and reflected that maybe he should stop drinking on a Sunday night as his head was feeling increasingly murky.

Phil had set himself a wee tradition on a Sunday night for the past three years. He loved all the sport on TV on a Sunday, especially the

Grand Prix. Sunday was his day. Habitually, he always got up around ten, went for a four mile run, then made himself a lovely roast dinner after his shower and before the sport started. This was accompanied by beer and wine, occasionally with the odd bottle of champagne, depending on how his week had gone. He didn't remember particularly overindulging last night, but by the way he felt this morning he must have. He felt like he'd been disturbed from an intensely deep sleep.

The Grand Prix was a legacy of his dad. They used to sit together watching it when he was a boy while Mum was in the kitchen cooking a roast dinner. Since his parents had been killed in a car crash a few years ago, he'd kept the tradition going. Not even the attentions of his beautiful Laura were enough to distract him from this convention.

He'd worked with Laura for a while and they'd recently become engaged. They'd both agreed on a long engagement and she was fine with his little Sunday *quirk*. He was meeting her for lunch later today and was going to surprise her with the arrangements he'd made for a romantic weekend away in the country. She always moaned he wasn't romantic enough and he was determined to prove her wrong.

Leaving the café behind him, he walked out into the glorious sunshine. People were rushing by. They seemed like amoebas to him: quickening to proliferate. He felt displaced. He thoughts, once clear, were misting. He stood in the street and held out his hands. People walked by him; rushing. He couldn't feel them bumping into him: he felt disconnected from his body and the sun was fogging his vision. He looked at the people propelling past him: the radiated light was making their eyes stick out and he could see their skulls beneath. Cheekbones protruded and teeth grinned; some shook with the effort of talking. Eyes disappeared as the hollows spoke. Skeletons chattered: a murmur of vacant bones clattering against concrete. The oozing light blinded his eyes as he felt himself drift into a fissure.

A horn broke his concentration as clarity snapped back. He jumped onto the pavement only to notice the crowd turning to look at a boy behind him who ran to his mum having avoided a car. The people returned to normal: vacuous souls flocking to work, their momentary distraction forgotten. Phil pressed his fingers to his temples to alleviate the gnawing resonance that was increasing at the back of his head. Momentarily relieved, he re-joined the hoarding masses.

At the end of the next street he entered his office block. It looked very different. The plants had been changed for larger ones and the décor didn't look quite as sharp. He punched the button for the elevator and smiled at the new guard on the door. When he didn't respond, Phil shook his head in irritation and wondered why people were so rude.

Walking away from the elevator on his floor, Phil knew that something was wrong. The carpets were different and he barely recognised anyone. He was confused as to how the place could change so much over the course of a weekend. With heavy feet, Phil walked the long corridor to his office: the gnawing in his head growing louder. His eyes became heavy as he dragged them upwards to look at the door. They widened inordinately when he saw the name there: Ian Cruickshank: his old colleague. He wondered why Ian's name was on his door and what had happened over the weekend to facilitate such changes. He pushed the door open and looked inside. Ian was sitting at his desk; his eyes widened when he saw Phil.

Phil's head screamed in agony and before he knew it he was outside again. The sun was bearing down on him and the raw noise in his head was increasing. He felt like his teeth were rattling and every movement was becoming a chore. Through his blurring eyesight he saw the man he had seen only an hour ago: the one who resembled his grandad. He was looking at Phil and pointing at something, Phil followed the direction of his signal.

He was walking on grass. There was a tent in front of him. He couldn't make it out. Every step was becoming profound; his eyesight growing more and more vague. There was a sign in front of the tent. He recognised it as a police sign and had to force his eyes to read it. He was finding it increasingly difficult to concentrate and the noise in his head was becoming unbearable. The sign said something about exhuming remains after five years' interment. Something to do with a murder inquiry. New leads requiring a new autopsy. Phil scarcely had time to wonder why the old man had pointed this out to him, when he fell through the tent and into the grave. As he fell through the earth, a diaphanous spirit, he barely registered his name on the plaque of the coffin before he landed in his decayed body and darkness prevailed.

On the other side of town in a swanky marble apartment, Ian placed the empty bottle of pills beside his confession letter. He felt sure he'd seen Phil's ghost at the office door today and he'd heard the murder investigation had reopened. He'd phoned Laura to warn her. What she did now was her business.

THE SCREAMING

Barry Woods

There is so much junk up here, I can't believe Mum kept all of this; hoards of paperbacks; magazines; board games - even my old school blazer. I take a gulp of tea and rummage through the boxes labelled *Tim.* Then I find it. The Kathy Vine record hides in a box of LPs. I pick it out and dust it off. Her elf-like face stares out from the cover sleeve and makes me shiver. I move to the window, see the derelict summerhouse poking its roof out from the orchard. I remember ...

I remember 1983 and that day in art class when Johnny Hayden saw something humorous in my painting of another world. I knew then he had the power to make my life a systematic hell.

'Carter's painted a load of stiff pricks - look!'

'No. They're towers,' I said.

'Hey, at least he has imagination,' Walshy called. Walshy was the bully's bully, Johnny's own nemesis.

At the end of the lesson, Johnny spilt his brush water over my picture, reducing my colony on Mars to a washed out mess.

'Oops. Sorry! I only meant to ...' he chuckled with Travo as they washed their brushes at the sink. I tried to blot it dry but it was useless: the orange paint crawled across the page and dripped off the edge, unsalvageable. I was furious. Mr Draper hadn't seen and continued to potter about in the corner, more nutty professor than art teacher.

After dinner, Johnny pursued me down the running track. He checked for any of my allies before wrenching my arm behind my back.

'Just give him a quick dig,' said Travo.

It was a painless effort. He did it again. 'Don't ever make a prick out of me!'

'Get off, Johnny.' It hurt this time.

'Hayden, what are you up to now, eh?' Johnny let go as Walshy strolled by. 'What are you doing?'

'Nothing.'

Walshy lunged at him and trapped him in a headlock. I stood back as Johnny's face turned purple. 'There's only one place for people like you.'

I hoped he wouldn't.

Walshy dragged him over to the corner and to the disused water hydrant that stuck out from the wall; the Hom Machine would certainly give you a bruised arse.

Johnny struggled. Walshy punched him in the shoulder before lifting him up by the lapels and shoving him against the device.

'Get off - I was just joking!'

'Leave the little ones alone. Got it?'

'Yes ... yes,' said Johnny.

Some of the other boys had gathered to watch just as there was a loud tear. Walshy let go. Johnny rubbed his backside and felt the rip in his trousers and the thinness of his exposed boxer shorts. The gang of black blazers and sports bags tittered like hyenas.

After school, I went into town and browsed the record shops; I picked up the latest Duran Duran and Kathy Vine albums. When I got home I had to endure Richard's preaching.

'I've told you about wasting your mother's money on this sort of rubbish. It will distract from your studies; we don't want you joining the back of the dole queue at 16 - well, your mother doesn't anyway.'

'Yeah, right,' I rolled my eyes.

'Better pull your finger out before it's too late, young man.' He liked to mock; his main concern was my younger brother David, his biological son, the one who would benefit from a private education.

I hurried up the stairs and played Duran Duran on the old record player. It was perfect pop. The Kathy Vine record was like nothing else I'd ever heard: a concept album called *The Screaming,* recommended to me by Andy Rowlands.

'Devil messages are hidden within the grooves,' he'd enthused. 'Try playing it backwards.'

Kathy Vine was diverse and experimental; I found her voice and the whole mood of the record sinister. Some tunes were mellow and soothing whilst others literally screamed. Track 5 had some incoherent lyrics that seemed to be warbling in reverse. I did what Andy had told me and played it backwards, and as the grooves fed under the stylus I heard a message. It was clever like a code. It sounded like, *'I ... let ... them ... in ... now. I ... let ... them ... in ... now.'* And then I saw something strange and intrusive, a reflection on the wall. It was a sphere of light that began to dart around in circles across the attic's exposed beams and then down onto my duvet. It was coming from the summerhouse. I thought it would be kids from the council estate messing about with a mirror or torch; they frequently got through the railings and invaded Richard's precious land. Worse still, it could be Johnny Hayden.

I crept down the springy lawn to see but when I got closer I realised it was too quiet. There were no noisy estate kids around. I went inside and stepped over the carpet of twigs and leaves that littered the stone floor. Then I saw her ... just a silhouette at first by the far window. It seemed she was a shadow, her colouring black - entirely black: her tumbling hair, her shiny skin, her veined moth-like wings. From the palm of her hand came the ball of light and she moved it up to her forehead, illuminating her face and reflecting into her beautiful almond-shaped eyes. She moved the glow towards me and it touched my brow. There was a warm tingle and I got an instant feeling of euphoria; I felt a connection as if she were gathering information from me telepathically. It lasted only a few seconds before she promptly withdrew. Her body then dispersed into thousands of fluttering particles and danced out of the window like a carnival of butterflies. I followed and watched them fade into the sky.

She was on my mind all the next day in school; I couldn't concentrate properly in maths; I wasn't even bothered when Johnny leered a face full of freckles at me.

That night I did the same thing, I played track 5 backwards until I heard those strange words. This time when I got down to the summerhouse there was no light and no black lady, though there were some unwelcome visitors. An apple hit me on the shoulder and as I turned I saw Johnny and Travo emerge from the orchard.

'Hey, posh boy,' said Johnny. 'Lend us a tenner.'

'Get out of the garden, Johnny, I mean it.'

'Will you tell Mummy and Daddy on us?' He threw another.

'Just get out of here.'

'I'll do whatever I like.'

'Go on, get him!' said Travo.

They ran at me and were soon punching and kicking me on the floor.

'You live in a mansion and you go to a comp!' I heard Johnny snigger as he gave me the imprint of his cheap shoe. 'Why aren't you in some posh school?'

I rolled around on the grass and kicked back at them. I planted a good one on Johnny's shin, which enraged him even more. Then, just when I expected to get a battering, something made them stop and they stared dead ahead. Johnny pointed. 'What is that?'

Out from the summerhouse came the black lady with the magical light held high above her head.

'It's a fairy,' he chuckled. 'Carter's got fairies at the bottom of his garden!'

They were intrigued ... until they heard grunting. I saw many sets of what looked like pigs' trotters shuffle out from under the trees. When they came into view, I saw they were little people, about four feet high, with floppy ears and glistening snouts. They brought an awful odour with them too. Johnny backed up closer to me. 'Pigs!' he said. 'Carter's got pigs in his garden!'

They looked like pig-boys standing upright on two legs dressed in ragged cloth. Their number increased; an endless, dirt-faced army emerged from the trees to surround us.

'Hah ... pigs ...' Johnny faltered. His expression turned sour. Johnny and Travo made a run for it but the pig-boys separated into groups and blocked their way. They squealed and grunted excitedly then picked up Travo and held him above their heads like a trophy. Johnny only made it a couple of yards before he too was caught. Then, charging to the summerhouse with their prisoners, they fought viciously to get through the narrow doorway. They scuffled so much I thought the bricks would collapse around them. When the last set of mucky trotters had gone inside, a silence fell over the orchard. Warily, I looked in. I saw emptiness. They had vanished into thin air ... or perhaps passed through into some other world. Only the silvery light remained, sparkling at head height like a disembodied firework.

Johnny and Travo never turned up for school.

After some months' investigating, the police decided the boys had endured disturbed home lives and had added themselves to the many thousands of runaways. I said nothing, of course, then I buried it mentally, piled the years on top like soil; I had no further issues with Johnny after buying the Kathy Vine record.

I'm surprised *The Screaming* is still here after twenty years. I slide the disc from its sleeve and move over to the record player. I place the record onto the turntable then drop the needle on track 5. It is crackly. I do the backwards thing again and Kathy's hidden message is clear once more. *'I ... let ... them ... in ... now. I ... let ... them ... in ... now.'*

I look through the window and see the signal. I go down the unkempt garden and head through a swarm of gnats to the building; the doorway is crumbling with dry rot now.

Inside I see she is no older; her wings twitch; she lifts the light to her forehead then to mine. I feel a surge of renewed youth: I feel the telepathic connection and then she seeks my thoughts just as she did years earlier. She returns the light to her head and in the blackness of those eyes, just for a second, I see the reflection of Richard at his desk in the city.

I pull out of the driveway curious about his will. The house shall be split equally between David and me in the event of his death ... or disappearance, a clause Mum insisted on. She passed away last month so I have nothing to lose by sending him a piece of my mind courtesy of Kathy Vine.

INFORMATION

We hope you have enjoyed reading this book - and that you will continue to enjoy it in the coming years.

If you are interested in becoming a New Fiction author then drop us a line, or give us a call, and we'll send you a free information pack.

Alternatively if you would like to order further copies of this book or any of our other titles, then please give us a call or log onto our website at www.forwardpress.co.uk